CULTURE SMART!
NAMIBIA

Sharri Whiting

916.81
WHITI

First published in Great Britain 2008
by Kuperard, an imprint of Bravo Ltd
59 Hutton Grove, London N12 8DS
Tel: +44 (0) 20 8446 2440 Fax: +44 (0) 20 8446 2441
www.culturesmartguides.com
Inquiries: sales@kuperard.co.uk

Culture Smart! is a registered trademark of Bravo Ltd

Distributed in the United States and Canada
by Random House Distribution Services
1745 Broadway, New York, NY 10019
Tel: +1 (212) 572-2844 Fax: +1 (212) 572-4961
Inquiries: csorders@randomhouse.com

Copyright © 2008 Kuperard

Series Editor Geoffrey Chesler
Design Bobby Birchall

ISBN 978 1 85733 473 9

British Library Cataloguing in Publication Data
A CIP catalogue entry for this book is available from the
British Library

Printed in Malaysia

This book is available for special discounts for bulk purchases
for sales promotions or premiums. Special editions, including
personalized covers, excerpts of existing books, and corporate
imprints, can be created in large quantities for special needs.

For more information in the USA write to Special
Markets/Premium Sales, 1745 Broadway, MD 6–2, New York,
NY 10019, or e-mail specialmarkets@randomhouse.com.

In the United Kingdom contact Kuperard publishers at the
address at the top of this page.

Cover image: Craft industry in Namibia. © Piccaya/Dreamstime.com
Images on pages 15, 32, 85, 88, 95, 96, 99, 101, 108, 119, 120, 131, 133, 137, and 160 by
courtesy of the author.
Images on the following pages by courtesy of Namibia Tourism at www.fotoseeker.com:
13, 14, 22, 24, 53, 71, 91, 105, 109, 122 and 163 (all © Ute von Ludwiger), 118, 123, 125,
126, 130, and 163.
Images on pages 21 © Ian Beatty; 35 and 126 © Thomas Schoch; 52 and 92 © Harald
Süpfle; 66 © Nick SS; 97 © Patrick Giraud; 102 © Eric Kristensen; 114 © FC Georgio;
121 © Hans Hillewaert; and 129 © Brian McMorrow.

About the Author

SHARRI WHITING is an international consultant and lecturer, with an MSc in communications management from Simmons College, Boston. Her work has taken her to the American University of Rome, Leiden University, the European School of Economics, and the University of Texas, among others. She has written widely on issues facing executives and dual-career couples working abroad.

Sharri spent four years in Namibia and has written about the country for Air Namibia's *Flamingo*, *Travel News Namibia*, and for major American publications. She was a guest lecturer at the University of Namibia, head judge for the Namibian Business Woman of the Year Awards, and a speaker before the Namibian Business and Professional Women's Association. She also writes about food, wine, and travel, and wrote the *Top Ten Guide to Rome* (2001). She is married to Piero De Masi, former Ambassador of Italy to Namibia. They live in Italy and the USA, and spend several weeks a year in Namibia.

**The Culture Smart! series is continuing to expand.
For further information and latest titles visit
www.culturesmartguides.com**

The publishers would like to thank **CultureSmart!**Consulting for its help in researching and developing the concept for this series.

CultureSmart!Consulting creates tailor-made seminars and consultancy programs to meet a wide range of corporate, public-sector, and individual needs. Whether delivering courses on multicultural team building in the USA, preparing Chinese engineers for a posting in Europe, training call-center staff in India, or raising the awareness of police forces to the needs of diverse ethnic communities, it provides essential, practical, and powerful skills worldwide to an increasingly international workforce.

For details, visit www.culturesmartconsulting.com

CultureSmart!Consulting and **CultureSmart!** guides have both contributed to and featured regularly in the weekly travel program "Fast Track" on BBC World TV.

contents

Map of Namibia	7
Introduction	8
Key Facts	10
Chapter 1: LAND AND PEOPLE	**12**
• Topography	12
• Political and Geographical Regions	13
• Climate	18
• Namibia and Its People	19
• Namibia as a Society	30
• A Brief History	32
• Natural Resources	35
• The Economy	38
• Namibia in Africa	43
Chapter 2: VALUES AND ATTITUDES	**46**
• Justice and Social Harmony	47
• Attitudes Toward Nature	48
• Religion	49
• Patriotism, Heroes, and Unifying Symbols	56
• Gender Relations	60
• Attitudes Toward Time	63
• Personal Space and Privacy	63
Chapter 3: BELIEFS, CUSTOMS, AND TRADITIONS	**64**
• Customs and Rituals	64
• Birth, Death, and Life Events	68
• Manners	72
• Holidays and Celebrations	73
Chapter 4: MEETING NAMIBIANS	**76**
• Couples Across Race and Culture	78
• Getting to Know Namibians	79
• Attitudes Toward Foreigners	80
• Meeting and Greeting	81
• Time in a Social Setting	81

• Invitations Home	83
• Appropriate Dress	85
• Dating and Making Friends	88

Chapter 5: THE NAMIBIANS AT HOME — **90**
• The Family	90
• Education	92
• Daily Life	95
• Medical Care	96
• Summer Vacations	96

Chapter 6: TIME OUT — **98**
• Eating and Drinking	99
• Supermarkets	105
• Dining Out	105
• Gambling and Nightlife	106
• Drinking, Smoking, and Drug Use	106
• Street Beggars	107
• Shopping For Pleasure	107
• Museums, Galleries, and Cultural Sites	114
• Music and the Performing Arts	116
• Sports	117
• Wildlife	118

Chapter 7: TRAVEL, HEALTH, AND SAFETY — **128**
• Border Crossings and Entry Requirements	128
• Getting Around	129
• Tours	135
• Where to Stay	136
• National Parks and Private Preserves	137
• Health	138
• Safety	139

Chapter 8: BUSINESS BRIEFING — **140**
• Government Policy	140
• The Business Community	142

contents

- Promoting Racial Diversity 144
- Women in Business 145
- Corruption 146
- Team Namibia 147
- Making Contact 148
- The Importance of Personal Relationships 148
- Dress Code 150
- Greetings 151
- Entertaining Business Colleagues 152
- Punctuality 153
- Meetings 154
- Contracts and Disputes 155

Chapter 9: COMMUNICATING 156
- Language 156
- Nonconfrontation and Respect 157
- Humor 157
- Body Language 158
- The Communications Revolution 159
- Technology 160
- The Media 161
- Mail 162
- The Impact of Diplomacy 162
- Conclusion 162

Appendix: Some Namibian Terms and Expressions 164
Further Reading 165
Index 166
Acknowledgments 168

Map of Namibia

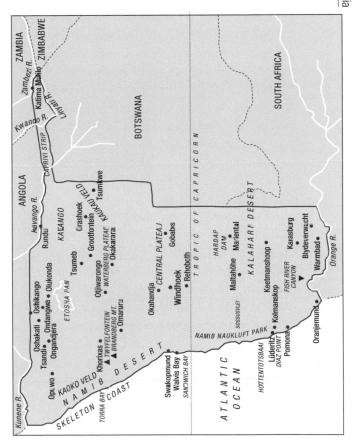

introduction

Imagine standing on a single spot in a land so vast
and empty that it is possible that no human being
has ever stood there before. You will experience
a magical sense of isolation, of empowerment,
of freedom, and of communion with the
environment. This is the key to understanding
Namibians, for it is both the celebration of their
natural surroundings and the challenge of living
in a harsh terrain that make them who they are.

With a huge landmass, Namibia's population is
one of the least dense on earth. A little more than
two million people, representing fourteen tribes,
races, and ethnic groups, share this land, which
has some of the most unusual natural resources in
the world. The majority live in the north, along
the Namibian-Angolan border, or in the center of
the country in the capital city of Windhoek. The
rest live on private and communal farms and in
the smaller towns dotted around the country.

Regardless of where they live and who their
ancestors were, Namibians have many things in
common, the most important being their
commitment to conservation of the country's
distinct and diverse topography: gravel plains
juxtapose with an ocean of sand dunes, edged by
the Namib and Kalahari deserts, punctuated by
forests and savannas, plateaus and mountain
ranges, and fringed by the Skeleton Coast.

Namibians take pride in their country, which only became an independent democracy in 1990. There is a strong sense of collaboration when it comes to daily life. The mix of cultures is reflected in the faces on the streets—Ovambo, German, South African, Chinese—as well as by the colorful traditional dress of the Herero and Himba, by German architecture, and South African food and wines. You will hear Oshivambo, Afrikaans, and German spoken, in addition to English.

Tribal and ethnic traditions are important, not only to those in the countryside, but also to city dwellers who want to pass their heritage on. In the cities, you will find modern buildings and state of the art technology, while in small towns or in the bush time seems to have stopped a hundred years ago—except that even in the most remote areas there may be cell phones and computers.

Namibians face the daily challenges of living with almost constant drought amid some of the most spectacular scenery on earth. They feel a mutual responsibility for each other, for wildlife, and for the land they occupy together. No matter where you are in the country, they will welcome you. If you are in trouble, they will help you. If you appreciate humor, they will laugh with you. And, if you respect this amazing place and take care not to do harm, they will be your friends.

Key Facts

Official Name	Republic of Namibia	
Capital City	Windhoek	Pop. 233,529 (2001 census)
Major Towns	Grootfontein, Katima Mulilo, Keetmanshoop, Lüderitz, Ondangwa, Okahandja, Oranjemund, Oshakati, Otjiwarongo, Rehoboth, Rundu, Swakopmund, Tsumeb. Walvis Bay is a major port.	
Area	318,251.6 sq. miles (824,268 sq. km)	The size of Texas and Louisiana combined
Location	Southwestern Atlantic coast of sub-Saharan Africa, bordered by Angola and Zambia to the north, South Africa to the south, and Botswana to the east	
Terrain	Varies from coastal desert to semiarid mountains and plateau	15% of the land reserved for national parks and conservation areas
Climate	There is a winter dry season (May to October) and a summer rainy season (November to April). Rainfall ranges from .78 inches (19 mm) along the hyperarid coast to 29.5 inches (750 mm) in the Caprivi Strip.	Temperatures vary between seasons and regions, from lows under 32°F (0°C) to highs above 122°F (50°C), and can fluctuate dramatically between day and night. There are about 300 days of sunshine.
Currency	Namibian dollar (N $1=100 cents)	The South African rand and the Namibian dollar are both legal tender in Namibia; the Namibian dollar is not accepted in South Africa.

Population	2.1 million (est. 2008)	Growth rate approx. 2.6% per annum
Ethnic Groups	Black 85–87%; white 6–8%; mixed race 7%	About 50% belong to the Ovambo and 9% to the Kavango ethnic groups. Other groups: Herero 7%, Damara 7%, Nama 5%, Caprivian 4%, San 3%, Baster 2%, and Tswana 0.5%
Language	English is the official language; other languages spoken include Afrikaans, German, and several Indigenous languages.	Tribal langs. incl. Bantu (Oshivambo, Otjiherero, Kavango, Tswana, Caprivians) and Khoisan (San/Bushmen and Nama/Damara).
Literacy Rate	81% (adults, 2003)	
Religion	75% Christian; the rest mostly animist	Small Jewish and Muslim communities
Government	Multiparty democracy, with a president serving a five-year term	Bicameral parliament: National Assembly and National Council
Media	State-owned TV channel with news broadcasts in English and at least one tribal language; one independent TV channel	Many radio stations in local languages; daily newspapers in English, German, Afrikaans, and local languages, as well as several weeklies
Electricity	220 volts, 50 Hz	
TV/Video	PAL system	
Telephone	Country code 264	
Time	GMT +2 hrs, CET + 1 hr	During daylight saving: GMT + 1, same as CET

chapter one

LAND &
PEOPLE

TOPOGRAPHY

Shaped like a fist with a pointing index finger,
Namibia is a huge country of some 318,246 square
miles (824,268 sq. km), dominated by the oldest
desert in the world, the Namib, which means "the
barren plain beyond the dunes." The country's four
permanent rivers, the Kunene, the Okavango, the
Zambezi, and the Orange, make up the borders; all
other rivers in Namibia are ephemeral, with flow
dependent on rainfall. There are four distinct
topographical regions: the Central Plateau, the
Namib Desert, the Eastern Lowlands, and the
Okavango and Caprivi area.

The Central Plateau, the highest part of
Namibia, has altitudes as high as 6,500 feet
(2,000 m). It runs generally north to south, with
hills and the best farmland.

The Namib Desert, west of the escarpment
that marks the edge of the Central Plateau, runs
995 miles (1,600 km) along the Atlantic Ocean,
and is known for its towering reddish sand dunes.

The Eastern Lowlands lie to the east of the
Central Plateau. The land slopes off gradually

before meeting the Kalahari Desert, with its vegetated dunes and broad stretches of sand.

The Okavango and Caprivi areas in the far northeast are mostly flat and verdant, with running rivers and high rainfall.

The three major vegetation zones are: desert (16 percent), home to unusual plants such as the *Welwitschia* and the quiver tree; woodland (20 percent), in the north central and northeast areas, including riverine land, where teak wood is plentiful; and savanna grasslands (64 percent), with plants such as camel thorn and mopane.

POLITICAL AND GEOGRAPHICAL REGIONS

After Independence in 1990, Namibia was divided into thirteen regions.

Omusati, Oshana, Ohangwena, Oshikoto (north)

The four Ovambo regions, previously designated Ovamboland during South African rule, are home to the majority of the population, many of them communal farmers. Communal farms have no fences and no individual ownership, but property is traditionally passed from generation to generation. The mostly flat landscape can become flooded in the rainy season, so the best time to visit is April or May. The two main towns, Oshakati and Ondangwa, are in the Oshana region. The three-city complex of Oshakati-Ongwediva-Ondangwa is the second-largest concentration of people after Windhoek. The Etosha National Park is in the south, near the German mining town of Tsumeb.

Kunene (northwest)

The Kunene is a favorite destination for tourists looking for remote areas. It is bordered on the west by the Skeleton Coast National Park, which can be accessed at Torra Bay. The regional capital is Opuwo. Within the Kunene is the UNESCO World Heritage Site at Twyfelfontein, where rock paintings are thought to be more than 10,000 years old. It is also home to the desert elephant and the seminomadic Himba tribe. It is informally called Kaokoland, after the previously designated South African homeland.

Kavango, Caprivi (northeast)

The regions of the finger of land known as the Caprivi Strip share a territory full of rivers and trees. Most of the Caprivi Strip is bordered by Angola to the north and Botswana to the south, but at the very tip, to the east of the Caprivi capital of Katima Mulilo, four countries come together—Namibia, Botswana, Zimbabwe, and Zambia. Both regions are known for wildlife, such as hippos, crocodiles, elephants, and more, as well as for their basket making. The capital of the Kavango is Rundu, home of the Kavango wood-carvers.

THE MYSTERY OF THE FAIRY CIRCLES

Fairy circles are round patches of bare sandy soil surrounded by plant life. Oddly, nothing grows inside the circle. These circles dot the grasslands, occurring in a broken belt from

south Angola to the Orange River, the border between South Africa and Namibia. Scientists have no explanation for how or why they were formed and have considered radioactive soil, termites, and toxic proteins left by poisonous plants. So far, no viable explanation has been found. According to the San/Bushmen, these circles were where their ancestors danced in ancient times and will be forever empty.

Erongo (west)

The major cities in this region are the coastal towns of Swakopmund and Walvis Bay. It is home to part of the Skeleton Coast park, Cape Cross seal reserve, the Brandberg Mountain, and the most important wetlands on the West African coast.

Otjozondjupa (central)

This region contains the Waterberg Plateau park, the Herero capital of Okakarara, the Bushman center of Tsumkwe, and the towns of Grootfontein and Okahandja.

Omaheke (east)

This area is mostly empty of people, except for the town of Gobabis.

Khomas (central)

A mountainous region centered on the capital city, Windhoek, approximately 5,000 feet (1,525 m) above sea level.

Hardap (south)

Home to part of the Namib-Naukluft National Park, including Sossusvlei, the Hardap dam and lake, and the towns of Mariental and Maltahöhe. Many Namas live in this region.

Karas (south)

The region contains the Fish River Canyon and the towns of Keetmanshoop and Lüderitz. The

Sperrgebiet, the restricted diamond area, is here, part of which has been incorporated into the Namib-Naukluft National Park.

Still in use informally today are the names of areas that reflect population makeup, which were established by the Odendaal Commission of South Africa in the 1960s as "homelands." These include Damaraland, Bushmanland, Kaokoland, and Hereroland.

The Red Line

Also known as the Police Zone Line, or the Veterinary Line, the Red Line cuts across north central Namibia. The Germans drew this line, which was the color red on early maps, to keep their colonists based in the south, where they could be protected and live by German law. The tribes who lived north of the line were not subject to German law and their lands were protected from encroachment. When the South Africans took over, they kept the red line as a veterinary line, prohibiting movement of cattle to markets in the south. They then recruited laborers from north of the line to work in the diamond and gold mines in South Africa, often obliging them to stay away from home for a year or more. The Red Line still exists today, preventing communal farmers from selling their cattle to South African or international markets because the area has not yet been declared completely free of foot-and-mouth and other diseases. In 2007, it was proposed to

move the line further north, closer to the Angolan border, within the next ten years, as part of the area is now disease free. It is estimated there are 1.3 million head of cattle north of the line, with 700,000 to the south of it. Changing the line will enable communal farmers, most of them black, not only to sell cattle for export, but also to provide Namibia with additional sources of meat.

CLIMATE

Namibia's climate is typical of a semiarid country, with droughts a regular occurrence. It is the driest country in Africa south of the Sahara. Much of the conversation in Namibia is about when the next rains will arrive, how heavy they will be, and where they will fall. Days are mostly sunny, warm to very hot, while nights are temperate to cool. Average summer day temperatures range from 75–93°F (20–34°C), dropping at night to around 64°F

(18°C), sometimes as low as 46°F (8°C). Average day temperatures in winter vary from 64–72°F (18–22°C), with nights at 32–50°F (0–10°C). There are about three hundred days of sunshine a year.

The cold Benguela current running up the Atlantic coast is the prime influence on Namibia's climate, reducing rainfall and causing the coastal fog, which may go inland as far as 85 miles (135 km). Wildlife in the desert has adapted by learning how to obtain water from the fog.

Namibia is the most arid country in Southern Africa —humidity can be less than 10 percent in the winter, but as high as 50 to 80 percent in the summer. Rain usually falls in the summer between October and May, with the main rainy season from January to March. Rainfall is usually caused by thunderstorms, which occur unevenly throughout the country. Average rainfall figures range from less than .78 inches (19 mm) along the coast to 13.7 inches (350 mm) in the central area and 27.5 inches (700 mm) in the far north. When rainfall is good, ephemeral rivers fill and may even reach the coast; when rain in the south is especially heavy, magnificent fields of lilies appear like magic in the desert.

NAMIBIA AND ITS PEOPLE

Namibian people are as diverse as the landscape and it is impossible to understand Namibian culture without looking at the various groups who make up the population.

The country's 2.1 million inhabitants have an enormous amount of space in which to live—there are, on average, fewer than six people per square mile (2.43 per sq. km)—yet history shows that often they jostled for the same land. Why? The answer lies in the dictates of Mother Nature and the sparse supply of water and good grazing land. In fact, the influence of environmental factors on traditional practices is still apparent today, with some tribes living in different ways from their cousins in other areas, where water may be in better supply. Descriptions of the lifestyles of Namibia's varied cultures should therefore be considered generalizations.

The Bushmen, or San

The people with the longest history in Namibia are the Bushmen, or San, who have inhabited Southern Africa for at least 20,000 years. A nomadic hunter-gatherer tribe, they left behind records of their wanderings as rock engravings and paintings at Twyfelfontein (now a UNESCO World Heritage Site) and other sites in Namibia. Pushed ever east into the desert by the arrival of other tribes, the Bushmen/San today are respected for their survival skills and in-depth knowledge of the bush.

The old system of Bushman/San leadership was based on lineage and favored a leader who was modest, egalitarian, and generous; today, owing to responsibilities outside the tribe (participating in national or regional councils, land boards, etc.), leadership demands a more aggressive, articulate posture.

Though many live in towns and are no longer nomads, some still hunt as their ancestors did, using poisoned arrows and cleverly made traps. The women still gather more than eighty plants in the bush for food. The Bushman/San people create delicate and beautiful jewelry using hand-honed ostrich-shell beads, seeds, and nuts. Personal ownership of land is unknown.

The Ovambo

The Ovambo people make up 50 percent of Namibia's population, although they came onto the scene later. An agrarian society, they settled in northern Namibia in the mid-1500s, having descended from the Bantu-speaking tribes of Central Africa. Most reside today along the Kunene River. Though lifelong rights of utilization are granted, personal ownership of land is unknown. Traditionally, Ovambos lead a subsistence lifestyle, practicing animal husbandry and growing maize crops. In fact, maize fields were often grown around a village, with the maize stalks forming a protective barrier. Inside, huts called *ongandjos* were erected using maize stalks, tree branches, and

clay. Nowadays, square houses are replacing the circular huts. The Ovambo have historically been a matrilineal society, with status coming from the mother's family, but they are moving toward a patrilineal framework, as more and more families are separated when younger members go off to work in the cities.

The Kavango

The Kavango, also Bantu speakers, came from the lakes of East Africa and arrived in northeast Namibia in the late 1700s. Many live along the Okavango River, in a more verdant part of the country, where they fish and raise cattle, maize, and a variety of crops. Because of the large trees, the Kavango became wood-carvers, and now supply many of the craft markets around the country with handmade animals, bowls, masks, and the like. Their lineage is traced through the female.

The Herero

The third Bantu-speaking tribe in Namibia is the Herero. They arrived in northern Namibia from East Africa in the mid-1500s as nomadic cattlemen. Eventually, most moved south to the urban centers of the country, while those who remained behind became the pastoralist tribe known as the Himba. The history of the Herero is a bloody one. After the Germans colonized Namibia in the late nineteenth century, the headmen sold so much land to the Germans that the people insisted that the chiefs take it back. The land itself was not "owned" by the Hereros in a legal or formal sense, but they had a long-standing concept of "our land." When the German farmers enclosed the grazing land and the Hereros no longer had grass for their cattle, they decided to fight back. They planned a massacre of German settlers, but were themselves decimated by the colonists. Today, those Herero who still live in the countryside are mostly cattle farmers, eating meat, but not fish.

Herero society is governed by two elements, the paternal (*oruzo*) and the maternal (*eando*). Traditionally, women have controlled movable property, such as cattle, and the laws of inheritance, while men have determined status, place of residence, and the selection of chiefs. The Herero Paramount Chief rules over all and represents groups within the tribe to the government.

Married Herero women are easily recognizable by their colorful Victorian dresses, introduced by the missionaries in the late 1800s, and their broad headpieces, tied to resemble the horns of a cow.

The Himba
Though the Himba live primarily in Namibia's most remote region, the far northwest, they are

increasingly well-known. The women, who wear ruffled cowhide skirts and whose hairstyles denote their marital status, are beautiful. They adorn their skin with a mixture of powdered ochre, spices, and fat, which not only protects them from

the sun, but also helps retain a youthful appearance. The Himba, who are dispersed within the 19,300-square-mile (50,000-sq.-km) Kaokoland (Kunene) region, are one of the last seminomadic tribes in Africa living in traditional villages. They raise cattle and goats and move their herds seasonally to find grazing land. Today, most Himba children go to school in towns like Puros, where they wear Western-style clothing during the school week; a few others are kept at home to help raise the livestock, a job some consider even more important than getting an education.

The Nama

The Nama, also known as Hottentots in South Africa and Khoikhol in Namibia, are smaller and lighter skinned than many other tribes. They moved into Namibia in the early 1500s from

Botswana, where they became hunter-gatherers and, along the Atlantic coast, fishermen. The Oorlam subgroup, who came up from South Africa to escape the colonization of the Cape, joined them in the early 1800s. An interesting offshoot of the Namas are the Topnaar, who subsist in the dunes by obtaining food and water from the !Nara plants. Today, most of the fourteen Nama tribes live in towns in the more southern and arid regions of the country, having sold prime pieces of their tribal land to the Germans to settle their debts. The tribes are differentiated by the women's makeup and clothing colors. Namas are a patrilineal society.

The Damara

The history of the Damara is a bit cloudy—some think they arrived from West Africa in the 1500s, while others believe they came much earlier. They were enslaved by the Nama centuries ago and their language today reflects a mix of Nama and original Damara. Originally hunter-gatherers, they were pushed by the Nama and Herero to the mountains of north-central Namibia. They habitually stole livestock from their enemies and, fearful of other tribes, would often visit water holes at night. Because their footprints would be found in the morning, they were called Dama, meaning "who walks here" in Nama, which the Germans eventually changed to Damara. Damaraland (18,147 sq. miles, or 47,000 sq. km) suffered huge game losses from poaching in the 1970s and '80s, which resulted in a game guard system and, in the twentieth century, the creation of the Save the Rhino Trust, as well as several Community Conservancies. They are now benefiting from tourism, owing to the volcanic landscape, ancient rock art, black rhino, desert elephant, and the highest peak in Namibia, the Brandberg, all located in Damaraland.

The Rehoboth Basters
The Rehoboth Basters, today approximately 72,000 people, have an interesting history. Evolving under patriarchal laws, the *Vaderlike Wette*, they are descended from the Afrikaner trekkers who fathered children by Nama (Khoisan) mothers. They consider themselves a separate community from other Colored (mixed race) groups in Namibia and are registered as Rehoboth Basters.

Between 1868 and 1871, a group of almost one hundred Baster families left the Cape Colony in South Africa and moved into Namibia. In 1870 they settled at the hot-water springs called Rehoboth. They governed themselves until 1990, under the "homeland" rules of *apartheid*, when Namibia became independent and they fell under the new national laws. Most Rehoboth Basters speak Afrikaans as a first language, but with their own pronunciation and dialect. Their traditional style of dress was that of the Afrikaner trekkers—wide-brimmed hats and long trousers for the men, and long dresses and bonnets (*kappies*) for the women, which are now worn only on special occasions. Today, many Rehoboth Basters work in trades and professions in the major cities and dress in business attire.

The Coloreds

Mixed race people, called Coloreds, live throughout Namibia, as they do in other parts of southern Africa. This designation is a throwback to the *apartheid* era in South Africa, when people of mixed race were not allowed to intermarry with whites. Today, Namibia's Colored population is approximately 50,000, most of them well educated and working in towns and cities in a variety of professions. They place a high value on their Afrikaner roots and speak pure Afrikaans (unlike the Rehoboth Basters, who have their own dialect). They are considered to be disciplined, punctual, and family oriented.

Afrikaners

The white population of Namibia includes about 70,000 Afrikaners, who are dispersed throughout the country and speak Afrikaans—devolved from the seventeenth-century Dutch dialect spoken by the early colonists in South Africa—as a first language. The name "Afrikaner" came from the belief of the white settlers in the Cape that they were indeed rooted in Africa; Namibia's Afrikaners for the most part "trekked" up from South Africa in the nineteenth and early twentieth centuries. Afrikaners are integrated into Namibian society and have contributed much to the country. Afrikaans cuisine is popular, especially the *braaivleis* or barbecue (commonly shortened to *braai*), which is a core menu item in almost every Namibian household.

Germans
German missionaries arrived in Namibia in the 1830s, but it was not until 1884 that Germany officially colonized the area, excluding Walvis Bay, which was already controlled by Britain. The Germans called the country Südwest Afrika and, although they lost it during the First World War, after ruling for only thirty years, they left an indelible mark on its architecture, infrastructure, cuisine, and traditions. Today, about 25,000 German-speaking Namibians live in the country, some seventh- or eighth-generation descendants of the early settlers.

In modern Namibia, there are two types of Germans: South-West Germans, who are mostly the older generation ("pre-Independence Germans"), and Namibian Germans, their children or grandchildren, who are more modern-thinking and who speak a more informal German than their parents. The Germans have contributed significantly to the development of Namibia and continue to play an important part in the society today. During Namibia's struggle for independence, a large number of young black Namibians were sent to East Germany to be educated and returned to take their places in society and government.

The British

The British presence in Namibia began in 1807, when the first missionary society arrived. Eventually, though the British did not wish to control the entire territory of South West Africa, they did annex the area surrounding the port of Walvis Bay in 1878. Their major contribution to today's Namibia has been the English language, which became the official language of the country at Independence in 1990. There are about 8,000 whites in Namibia who speak English as their mother tongue, including some who do not have British ancestry, but are descendants of Italians, Portuguese, French, and others who settled here. The Etosha Pan was discovered by the English explorer Sir Francis Galton and his Swedish colleague, Charles John Andersson.

Caprivians

Other populations in Namibia include the almost 90,000 Caprivians, who live at the eastern end of the 7,722 square miles (20,000 sq. km) of the Caprivi Strip and are descendants of several tribes who came from South Africa and Zambia. The Caprivi is surrounded by rivers, and Caprivians are fishermen as well as agriculturalists. This population is known for making beautiful clay pots and baskets, and there are now organizations to help local craftspeople get their goods to market in the major centers.

Other minorities include the growing Chinese and other Asian populations, who have come to Namibia to do business, either privately or with the government. Jews and Indians are well represented in business and industry. There is a small Tswana population (Bantu speaking) living along the Namibia-Botswana border.

NAMIBIA AS A SOCIETY

Namibia is a country characterized by sharp economic inequality, with the wealthiest 1 percent consuming more than the entire less advantaged half of the population, many of whom do not yet have electricity or telephones. The richer people of all races live in expensive neighborhoods, speak English, send their children to private schools, travel to South Africa, Europe, and the US, and drive luxury cars.

Land Rights and Tribal Differences

More than half the economy is driven by agriculture and most of the population is engaged in farming. It is therefore an agrarian society overall, with profound cultural and social implications for all Namibians. Most indigenous farmers lost their land during the Colonial Wars (1904–07); land reform was promised by the government at Independence and has mostly been operated on a "willing seller, willing buyer" basis, with the government having first rights to purchase land that goes up for sale. A small number of farms, usually owned by absentee owners, has been appropriated by the government to reapportion to poor black farmers. Absentee landowners are charged a higher tax rate than resident ones.

Whites own most of the large businesses and commercial farms, though this is beginning to change as blacks and other nonwhites have entered the business sector and higher social classes. (The communal farms, mostly in the north, are run by a million blacks who share two-fifths of the fertile land in Namibia and live at a subsistence level—this is discussed further in the section on the economy.) In the public sector, the races are on more equal terms, but tribal differences often play a part in informal hiring practices. In rural communities, education plays a role in what social class people belong to, with teachers, government employees, businessmen and women and civil servants at the top. Despite this, there is always an underlying loyalty to family and local tradition.

A BRIEF HISTORY

Namibia's geographical features have had a great impact on its history. Survival has always been dependent upon water, and both man and animal have been forced to adapt to harsh conditions.

When the first Portuguese navigator, Diego Cao, planted his cross at Cape Cross in 1486, the territory was very sparsely populated. It is possible he saw no one; certainly, the desert coastline he encountered did not encourage him to stay and he quickly sailed on. Two years later, his countryman Bartolomeu Dias planted a second cross in the bay of Angra Pequena to the south, where Lüderitz is today; he, too, left quickly.

By that time, the Bushmen had been in Southern Africa for 20,000 years or more, and other tribes were just arriving from the north and

south. It would be more than three hundred years before European missionaries arrived in Namibia to establish mission stations at Warmbad and Blydeverwacht in 1805. The territory was called South West Africa (Südwest Afrika by the Germans), the name it kept until Independence.

Namibia became a German protectorate in 1884, by proclamation of the German Chancellor

Otto von Bismarck. Germany had come late to
the European land grab for African territories,
and it was thought it had not
acquired prime property until
diamonds were discovered in
Namibia in 1908. In order to
control vital river access to the
interior, particularly to its
colony in East Africa (now
mainly in Tanzania), Germany
negotiated with Britain for the
rights to the northeastern
finger of land known as the
Caprivi Strip. The Germans
were not able to annex the

Walvis Bay area, however, and the town and port
were only ceded back to Namibia by South Africa
after Independence.

As a result of the conquest of South West
Africa by South Africa, acting on behalf of the
British Empire during the First World War, the
administration of Namibia passed to South Africa
in accordance with a 1920 League of Nations
mandate. For the next forty years, South Africa
controlled Namibia, instituting *apartheid* policies,
some of which (the laws against interracial
marriage and the requirement that blacks live
separately from whites) were abandoned in
Namibia in the late 1970s, long before their
dissolution in South Africa; however, the *grand
apartheid* (including lack of voting rights for

blacks) continued until the eve of Independence. Many blacks continued to live along the northern border, where the majority of Namibia's population still resides today; the ruling South Africans also created segregated townships for resettlement of urban blacks. One such is Katutura outside Windhoek, the capital city.

In 1966, war broke out between the South African forces and the South West Africa People's

Organization (SWAPO), led by Sam Nujoma. Politically active blacks and some liberal whites were forced into exile; some went to New York to lobby the United Nations for assistance, others went to Europe and the Soviet Bloc to study, and others ended up in prison on Robben Island with Nelson Mandela. During the war, much of the

SWAPO activity was carried out from bases hidden in Angola.

In 1989, the implementation of UN Resolution 435 calling for free and fair elections resulted in SWAPO assuming control of the government. On March 21, 1990, Namibia became an independent country after a hundred and six years of foreign rule and Sam Nujoma became its first president. Almost fifty countries opened embassies and sent ambassadors in a show of support for the fledgling nation. In 1990, President Nujoma and his government pledged a program of National Reconciliation, which was later emulated by the Mandela government in South Africa. They declared English as the national language and implemented English instruction in schools throughout the country. They introduced the Namibian dollar shortly thereafter.

President Nujoma stepped down in 2005 after serving three five-year terms and was succeeded by Hifikepunye Pohamba.

NATURAL RESOURCES

Namibia's greatest resources and tourist assets are its wildlife and biodiverse environment. Large game found in the country include elephant, rhino, giraffe, buffalo, lion, leopard, and cheetah; there are about half a dozen species of antelope and thirty species of lizard in the Namib Desert. More than 630 bird species have been identified in the country.

There are 120 different tree species and 200 plant species. The *Welwitschia mirabilis*, one of the oldest plants on earth, can stay alive for as long as 2,000 years or more. Another remarkable plant is the quiver tree (*Aloe dichotoma*), which grows in southern Namibia, reaching

heights of up to 16.4 feet (5 m). It is said that the San/Bushman used the spiky leaves of the quiver tree to make quivers for their arrows, hence the name.

Namibia's incredible landscapes vary from dune "oceans" to broad savanna, the most arid desert, and craggy mountain ranges. There are vast mineral resources, including some of the world's best diamonds, a variety of gemstones, uranium, copper, lead, zinc, magnesium, silver, gold, granite, marble, and more. Preservation of wildlife and the environment must be balanced with obtaining the mineral riches underground.

The Atlantic coastline is known for its undersea diamonds and a large gas field, and for its oysters, fish, and shellfish. The main species, found in abundance off Namibia, are pilchards (adult sardines), anchovies, hake, and horse mackerel (scad), and there are smaller quantities of sole, squid, deep-sea crabs, rock lobsters, and tuna.

Preservation of the Environment
Namibia was the first country to include preservation of the environment in its constitution, and almost 15 percent of public lands are reserved for preserves and parks, all of which are managed by the Ministry of Environment and Tourism (MET). The protection of rare and endangered species was initiated in 1972 with the proclamation of Waterberg Plateau Park as a sanctuary and

breeding ground for the white rhino, eland, buffalo, and roan and sable antelopes. In the early 1980s, action was taken to protect the black rhino in the west and today Namibia is one of the few countries in Africa with an increasing population of black rhino. Because of the country's fragile environment, the focus on current and future tourism development is based on high-quality tourism with low numbers of visitors. Ecotourism activities with a minimal impact on the environment are imperative and have become popular with tourists.

In addition to the conservation activities of the MET, there are a number of NGOs engaged in conservation efforts, among them Namibia Nature Foundation, Integrated Rural Development & Nature Conservation, Save the Rhino Trust, Cheetah Conservation Fund, AfriCat Foundation, and AfriLeo Foundation. Private game ranches and lodges are committed to preservation of particular species on their properties.

Locally based conservation efforts involve conservancies, which allow the local population to become involved in conservation and preservation activities. In addition to protecting the environment and wildlife, conservancies also allow the indigenous population to share income and resources emanating from tourism.

Of the fifty conservancies registered, there are two types: those on commercial farmland (freehold conservancies) and communal conservancies, located on traditional communal and tribal lands. Their purpose includes the practice of sustainable conservation. Often, communal conservancies go into partnership with private enterprises, which provide management expertise for tourism projects. Proceeds are shared among bona fide land occupiers.

Desertification is Namibia's most urgent environmental issue; others are deforestation, overgrazing, bush encroachment, and loss of ground water resources.

THE ECONOMY

In 2006, Namibia achieved a GDP growth of 4.5 percent—relatively high for a developing country. The International Monetary Fund predicted 4.6 percent DPB growth in 2008. Namibia's non-oil producing neighbor, Botswana, was expected to achieve 5.0 and 5.2 percent respectively, and South Africa 4.7 and 4.6 percent. Angola, on the other hand, as an oil-producing country (Namibia is classified as a resource intensive country), was expected to experience 23.1 percent growth in 2007 followed by 27.2 percent in 2008.

Namibia's primary industries are agriculture, diamonds and other mining, tourism, fishing, and fish processing. In 2006, the inflation rate was approximately 6.1 percent. The Namibian Stock Exchange listed 27 companies at the end of 2006, with a market capitalization of N $1.059 billion.

The Namibian economy has a modern market sector, which produces most of the country's wealth, and a traditional subsistence sector. This reflects the SWAPO government's decision to move away from its revolutionary origins and embrace free market principles. Though there is a strong policy on training in place, the country still has one of the most unequal income distributions on the African continent. Increasing investment by the Chinese has resulted in additional employment opportunities for Namibians, though Chinese companies often bring in many of their own workers. The majority of Namibia's population depends on subsistence agriculture and herding; however, the country has more than 200,000 skilled workers, as well as a small, well-trained professional and managerial class.

More than 80 percent of Namibia's imports come from South Africa, and many Namibian exports are destined for the South African market, or transit that country. Outside South Africa, the EU (primarily the UK) is the chief market for Namibian exports, which consist mainly of diamonds and other minerals, fish products, beef and meat products, grapes, and light manufactures.

Health and education receive the largest financial share of the national budget, with the state goal of improving school graduation rates to 90 percent.

Tourism is one of the fastest-growing sectors in the Namibian economy, contributing about 16 percent to the GNP overall, and is expected to play a larger role in reducing the 37 percent unemployment rate, especially among the rural poor, who are increasingly involved in wildlife management and nature conservation, from which they can earn a living. In 2005, 777,890 tourist arrivals were logged; the industry is growing by approximately 12 percent a year, in keeping with the rate of tourism growth in southern Africa.

Because of Namibia's fragile environment and vast territory, marketing efforts are focused on individuals and small groups—high-quality rather than mass-market tourism—leading to an increase in luxury-level accommodation and facilities.

The mining industry in Namibia is affected greatly by currency exchange rates; non-diamond mining revenues represented more than 50 percent of total exports in 2004 (gold, uranium, copper, and zinc).

Namibia's diamond industry produces very high quality diamonds and employs more than 4,000 people. Offshore diamond mining began in the 1990s and 2007 marked the recovery of one million carats' worth from the Atlantic Ocean; a similar number of carats was mined on land. The government has established the Namibia Diamond Trading Company, which will allow a percentage of local diamonds to be cut, polished, and sold in Namibia, rather than sent to the Central Selling Organization in London. This is expected to increase skill levels of Namibians in this field, and improve the profitability and competitiveness of the local mining industry. (Visitors should avoid purchasing diamonds and other protected resources outside licensed retail establishments. The penalty for illegal dealing in diamonds in Namibia is stiff—up to US $20,000 in fines or five years in prison—and the courts generally impose the maximum sentence.)

Sparkling Chicken

A woman who grew up in the region of Namibia near Lüderitz and the Sperrgebiet (the zone controlled by the diamond industry, into which entry was forbidden other than by employees, who were rigorously searched before leaving) recalled that in the early 1930s her grandmother killed a chicken for dinner and discovered a diamond inside it. Obviously, it had pecked the ground for food and swallowed the diamond. According to family lore, after the incident was reported to the authorities, they slaughtered all the chickens and forbade the consumption or the keeping of fowl for some years for fear another diamond might be found and not turned in.

The clean, cold waters off the coast of Namibia are home to some of the richest fishing grounds in the world. Commercial fishing and fish processing are among the fastest-growing sectors of the Namibian economy in terms of employment, export earnings, and contribution to GDP. In addition to the important fishing industry centered on the Atlantic coast (with a harvest of more than 500,000 metric tons), Namibia has embarked upon aquaculture in the Zambezi/Chobe river systems with a view to establishing fish farming as a viable industry and employer in the north.

Agriculture utilizes about 170 million acres (70 million hectares) of land in Namibia and contributes the most to GNP, as well as providing the most employment. Of the land used for agriculture, 52 percent is for raising cattle (usually fed naturally, without added hormones), while small stock farmers utilize 33 percent; only 1 percent of this land is arable.

The agriculture sector has been divided into commercial and communal farming since colonial times. Both German and South African administrations subsidized white farmers, while denying land to blacks. Today, there are approximately 4,000 commercial farms, usually 12,000 to 24,000 acres (5,000 to 10,000 hectares) in size, with prosperity dependent upon available water—a small percentage of these have been purchased by blacks since Independence in 1990. Communal farms (most often raising cattle and goats) are operated at a subsistence level by about one million Namibians on small plots of shared land owned by the state.

NAMIBIA IN AFRICA

Since 1990, the country's executive has been headed by the president (elected for a five-year term) and the prime minister. There is a bicameral parliament, consisting of the National Assembly and the National Council. The judiciary consists of the Supreme Court, the High Court,

and the lower courts. On Independence, the country was divided into thirteen administrative regions.

There is universal adult suffrage in Namibia. The major political parties include the South West Africa People's Organization (SWAPO), the Democratic Turnhalle Alliance (DTA), the United Democratic Front of Namibia (UDF), the Congress of Democrats (COD), the Republican Party (RP), the National Unity Democratic Organization (NUDO), and the Monitor Action Group (MAG).

In 1990, the new government embarked on a program of national reconciliation and democracy, which has been recognized by its neighbors and the rest of the world as a courageous, nonviolent alternative to what could have been a policy of retribution. It is thought that when Nelson Mandela came to power in South Africa in 1994 he had been inspired by the Namibian model. Certainly, on several occasions, he visited Namibia and met former fellow prisoners from Robben Island who had been part of the Namibian Independence Movement.

Although SWAPO in exile had been a party of revolution, it adopted a policy of enlightened self-interest. Its undeniable majority (Ovambos, the largest tribe in Namibia, make up much of SWAPO's membership) gave it *carte blanche* to

choose any direction: however, wiser heads knew that to continue to receive the political and financial support of the West required them to moderate any authoritarian Marxist leanings. Certainly, this decision was helped along by the world situation in 1990, with the crumbling of the Soviet Union and the end of the Cold War.

Namibia is a member of the Southern Africa Development Community (SADC) and the African Union, as well as international organizations such as the UN, the Non-Aligned Movement, the Group of 77, and the British Commonwealth. It served as chair of the SADC committee on Politics, Defense, and Security Cooperation, and is a member of the African Union Committee of Ten on UN reform. Offices of the Southern African Customs Union and Eastern and Southern Africa Management Institute are located in Windhoek.

Namibia is committed to achieving the 15 percent health care budget allocation target set at the African Heads of State and Government Summit in 2000; other projects include implementation of the SADC Free Trade Area agreement, and cooperating with South Africa and Angola on infrastructure and activities surrounding the 2010 World Cup and the Africa Cup of Nations. It is also discussing visitor access to wildlife parks and areas that cross international borders; and is creating linkages between its own economic centers and harbors and those of neighboring countries including the construction of transport corridors such as the Trans Kalahari, Trans Caprivi, and Trans Kunene highways.

As a stable country, Namibia is home to almost 7,500 asylum seekers from other African countries, such as the Democratic Republic of Congo, Zimbabwe, and Angola.

chapter **two**

VALUES & ATTITUDES

As we have seen, Namibia is primarily an agrarian society, in which lives, both black and white, revolve around agriculture, weather, and the seasons. This is often the common denominator in a country of so many varied cultures. There is a shared pride in Namibia's landscape and resources, as well as a commitment to conservation that is rooted in ancient tribal laws and customs. There is also the embrace of traditional African values, including respect for others and the necessity of sharing nature's bounty with others.

As a rule, Namibians have a strong work ethic and are extremely self-reliant. Life expectancy is shorter than in Western countries and people expect to feed themselves by their own labor until they are too old to do so. As a Nama man working on the highway in a remote area said, "We believe it is necessary to finish all the work and then to rest. We must not have people sitting around in the sun."

Confrontation is not the preferred way of resolving disputes and loud voices and arguments are rarely heard, at least not in public. People are generally easygoing.

JUSTICE AND SOCIAL HARMONY
Customary vs. Common ("White Man's") Law

Traditional tribal courts have always been a fundamental part of Namibia's system of justice. To most tribes, justice means *restoration* and, therefore, most customary law sanctions levied to right wrongs are by way of compensation, sometimes called "wiping the tears." The starting point for these courts is the idea of one-for-two: if you steal one cow, you pay back two. The traditional courts aim to achieve results that are understood and accepted by the people's concept of justice.

In Africa in general, customary law is considered to be flexible, not rule-driven, and is focused upon the restoration of social harmony. In Namibia after Independence, the common law put in place by South Africa was gradually rewritten to accommodate traditional tribal law in certain circumstances. This was because procedures can be conducted in the local language; traditional courts are more efficient than state courts; and traditional courts are cheaper than state courts.

Thus, the Traditional Authority of the Kavango tribe (Laws of the Mbukushu) assesses the payment of fines in cattle according to the severity of the transgression: the penalty for illegal hunting (poaching) is two head of cattle, whereas for burning the *veld* (savanna) it is five head of cattle.

In the Kaokoland area of northwestern Namibia, fines for picking unripe fruit or destroying young mopane worms are payable in sheep and goats.

Those under the Gciriku Traditional Authority were not allowed to hunt animals with long noses, which were reserved for the *hompa* (tribal chief)—anyone caught hunting giraffes or hippos would be fined fifteen head of cattle.

The Ondango (Ovambo) culture's traditional law regarding widows became a nationwide point of reference and was reconfirmed by the state in 1993: widows are allowed to stay on the land they occupied during the time of their marriage without additional payment.

ATTITUDES TOWARD NATURE

Nature is the overarching concern of most Namibians, whether they are farmers, campers, conservationists, or simply want to water the garden. There is a great respect for the environment, as well as a single-minded concern for water. Do not waste water if you visit Namibia—it is a precious commodity. Integral to the African worldview is a belief that man and nature are intertwined and this belief is shared by most Namibians, regardless of race, tribe, or origin.

Many traditional laws are concerned with conservation, hunting, and preservation of wildlife and plants, though many rules were not needed in the past when wildlife, trees, and other natural resources were abundant. (After German colonization, trophy hunting decimated many herds, which have been reestablished since Independence.) In the past, hunting rituals and ceremonies played an important part in the conservation of wildlife (see Chapter 3); today natural resources are protected by common law, which has established "human free" zones (national parks) and provided an efficient system of regulation of natural resources. Today, there is a strong government ministry, the Ministry of Environment and Tourism, that works hand in hand with the people to promote and protect the environment.

RELIGION

The traditional African view of the universe integrates the spiritual and the physical worlds and has a direct bearing on everyday life. There is a belief in the spiritual interconnectedness of all living things; unlike much of Western religious thought, the African worldview regards the spiritual as much a part of life as the physical. While traditional Christianity distinguishes between good and evil, exemplified by the fall from grace of Adam and Eve, the African view is that goodness can be found in everyone—a more humanist approach. There is a strong sense of harmony with nature and the importance of the survival of the group. Change is seen as cyclical and natural; all events are interconnected. Africans invariably look to a higher power for strength and inspiration.

Christianity

Today in Namibia, about 90 percent of the people profess to be Christian, with the remainder primarily animists. Yet, there continue to be rituals and traditions practiced that conflict with Christian doctrine.

Christianity has helped to shape Namibian life in both positive and negative ways. The effect of the arrival of European missionaries in the nineteenth century can be seen today in the colorful Victorian dresses over heavy petticoats worn by married women of the Herero tribe, and in the changed attitude toward women, introduced by the Church, that resulted in the diminution of their power. Christian doctrine at the time was patriarchal and puritanical, as well as conservative about sexual issues.

The missionaries imposed a patriarchal view upon tribes where previously women had held positions of importance. Traditional ceremonies marking a girl's marriageability in many tribes (called *ohango* in Oshivambo) were also affected by the arrival of Christianity: the *lobola* changed from a bride price, usually paid in cattle, to an elaborate and expensive church wedding ceremony.

THE AFRICAN WAY
In the early 1990s, an Italian priest, long
assigned to southern Namibia and ministering
to many Namas, was made a bishop. The
consecration ceremony was held in a football
stadium on a very hot sunny morning and
thousands of people were there, most of them
Namas. At least a dozen African bishops were in
attendance, and they sat upon a stage erected for
the day, resplendent in their robes of varying
reds. Most were black men, although one or two
were white; there was also a representative of the
Vatican, a movie-star handsome prelate who
wore obviously hand-tailored vestments.

The ceremony was long, but very moving.
There were liturgical dancers, beautiful young
Nama women who danced sensuously to the
religious music. Next came a promenade of
priests and a variety of Namas wearing eclectic
patchwork costumes, who marched around the
track singing and dancing. The choirs sitting in
the stands began to sing, their music soaring to
the cloudless blue sky, the people swaying to the
complex African harmonies:

> Good news, wonderful news of God.
> Good news, wonderful news,
> Wonderful news of God.

Then in clicking Nama:

> !Gai #hoas buruxa #hoas, buruxa #hoas
> !Khub dis.
> Buruxa #hoas, !Khub dis.

... all to the tune of "Where Have all the
Flowers Gone?"

Some say Christian doctrine has actually reduced marriage rates (because young, often unemployed men cannot afford to pay for it) and has resulted in a very high incidence of births out of wedlock.

The white population is primarily Dutch Reformed (Calvinist), though there are communities of Catholics, other Protestants, and Jews. In addition, there is a Muslim community in Windhoek.

Other Religious Beliefs

Many tribes, while professing and practicing Christianity, still perform traditional rituals and retain historic beliefs. The Ovambo, Namibia's largest population group, is primarily Christian, although Kalunga, the higher being previously worshiped, is sometimes called upon, as are the spirits of ancestors. Ovambos believe they share a common ancestor and identify with a totem, usually an animal or plant.

The Kavango believe in a supreme being named Karunga, who lives in heaven in the east of the sky. Karunga dictates nature in the form of wind and rain. There is also a powerful evil being named Shadipinyi, who takes the form of a lion or horned animal with a red tail and red nails, or of a man with horns. He brings death and tempts people into sin.

The Hereros formed a new Church in 1955, the Oruuano, which some say is an offshoot of the Lutheran Church, while others maintain it combines Christianity with ancestor worship and a bit of traditional magic. Though today many Hereros have returned to mainstream Christianity, there is still a respect for the supreme being called Ndjami, and a tradition of tasting the sacred milk from the holy cattle, the *ozohikirikwa.*

The Himbas believe in Mukuru as the creator of all things. Himbas reach Mukuru by praying to their ancestors, something that can only be done by men The Himbas, as well as other tribes, keep a holy or ritual fire (called *oruzo* by the Himbas) burning in the center of the village to represent the link between living and ancestral spirits.

Many Namas are Christian, in particular Roman Catholics. Still, some traditional beliefs remain in their culture. Two gods are worshiped, a good one and an evil one; ancestral spirits are also worshiped.

FOLK WISDOM

Here are some Ovambo sayings that reflect attitudes widely shared by many Namibians:

Omukintu ontungwa, "A woman is a basket"— meaning a woman never walks around without carrying a basket; she is resourceful.

Uukadhona omwede, "Girlhood has its own master"—a young girl is responsible for and to herself.

Ino mange ondjupa, ongombe inayi vala, "Do not get the churn ready before the cow has borne its calf"—don't count your chickens before they hatch.

Ondjala yopela kay'ehama ondjuulukwe okamana, "Hunger pangs are not painful; longing kills"—longing has a negative effect and makes one thinner than hunger.

Kahola omutoye, nakufu omutoye, "The first fruits are sweet, but so are the autumn fruits"—the first child is as special to the parents as the youngest.

Ohaa fululula iilambo iikulu, "They are digging old holes again"—they are digging up old disputes.

Kwa kukuta, oko ku nonkenya, "The hard thing has a seed in it"—when one perseveres, prosperity comes.

Ongundja ihuy' ende nakaanda, "The grain does not carry a larder"—one cannot carry one's wealth around with oneself.

Okulonga uuwanawa ompunda yomagadhi omatoye, "Doing good is a honeycomb" —the person who is kind to others has many friends.

Enongonongo kalu vulu, "A parasite cannot live on its own"—no person wants to live alone.

Aakulu taa siluka, aape taa tumbu, "The old go down and the young rise"—time and the world move on.

Uulelekule wa ndjila, "Endless road"—if I had been closer to you I would have arrived on time.

Namukaga gwaa li ombwa, "A dog is not killed by eating without oil"—a man is not killed by gossip.

Lya ka kali nuukali na nkombwena, "A goat that is old does not spare a young goat"—a man has no empathy for a child not his own.

Ke hoole okunyangadhala, na ki ifala komukodhi omunene, "He who likes to wander places himself in the claws of a hawk"—those who wander aimlessly find disaster.

Omeva ihaelinjenge ehena kapuka, "Water does not ripple without an insect"—a person always has a reason for becoming angry.

Omkeli kaj oondoza ji etele iikulja, "Peace fattens more than food"—peace is more beneficial than food.

Eno limwe kali tsakana hambo, "One tree is not enough to build a fence"—one person alone cannot alleviate poverty in a country.

The San/Bushmen also seek out the spirits of the dead, who are thought to have great power over the living in both positive and negative ways. Some San see the moon as the place where the ancestral spirits live. Animism, the belief that everything possesses a soul or spirit, is a great part of the San/Bushman belief system.

The Damara are now mostly Christians, although some still follow the Damara god []Gamab and ancestral spirits. []Gamab supplies water and food and, in the Damara language, the word means "water." A ritual fire, dedicated to the ancestors, is kept burning by the great wife of the village, a custom that may have come from the Herero.

PATRIOTISM, HEROES, AND UNIFYING SYMBOLS

The Republic of Namibia is a young country, and its unifying symbols are especially important in fostering and maintaining shared values and common goals. The constitution stipulates that the country have a national flag, a coat of arms, a national anthem, and a national seal, all of which serve to unify it.

The flag is rectangular with a red bar, bordered in white, running from the lower left corner to the upper right, and

representing the Namibian people, their heroism, and their determination to build a future with equal opportunity for all. Above the bar is a golden sun (representing life, energy, and the Namib Desert) on a field of blue (the sky, the ocean, the importance of rain); below the bar is a solid field of green (vegetation and natural resources).

The coat of arms is centered, with a shield bearing the same colors and design as the flag. Two oryx support the shield, and a fish eagle stands atop a band of six diamonds. The national motto, "Unity, Liberty, Justice," is written across a banner on the bottom, beneath a compartment featuring a Namibian sand dune and the *Welwitschia mirabilis* plant in the foreground. The national seal is similar to the coat of arms, but is designed to be printed in black and white or blind embossed. The motto and the name "Namibia" are located within a double circular border. In addition, there is a president's flag, which features three triangles (blue, yellow, green) and the coat of arms. This flag may only be used in Namibia.

Heroes

Namibia has recognized heroes from all walks of life and all ethnic groups. Heroes of the struggle for independence include Sam Nujoma, the first president and beloved "father" of the country;

Anton Lubowski, a white SWAPO activist, and Herero Chief and DTA president, Clemens Kapuuo.

An outdoor monument called Heroes' Acre, located six miles (10 km) south of Windhoek, commemorates those who died fighting for independence. Provision has been made for 174 resting places, of which nine are purely symbolic.

Kaptein Hendrik Witbooi: the Captain of the IKhowesin or Witbooi Nama. In 1890 he initiated the resistance struggle against the German colonizers.

Captain Jacob Marenga: a Herero leader in the Bondelswart rising against the Germans in 1903.

Chief Kahimemua Nguvauva: an early-twentieth-century Herero chief who fought the Germans and was eventually executed.

Chief Samuel Maharero: Supreme Chief of the Herero people who led his tribe in the bloody war with the Germans in 1904, in which 64,000 of the 80,000 Hereros were killed.

Chief Nehale Iya Mpingana: Ondonga tribal leader who fought the Afrikaner trekkers and German imperial forces between 1886 and 1904 and successfully blocked the declaration of Namutoni area as the "Republic of Upingtonia" by the colored South African trader William Worthington Jordan and twenty-five other Dorsland Trekker families.

Chief Mandume ya Ndemufayo: King of Ovamboland who commited suicide during an attack by the South Africans in 1917 rather than be killed or captured; he was an inspiration to anti-colonial fighters.

Chief Ipumbu ya Tshilongo: resisted the influence of missionaries over his people, the Ovakwambi, but later became an outcast because his tribe refused to be associated with him.

Chief Hosea Kutako: Herero chief who participated in the German–Herero War in 1904 and regarded as the father of Namibian nationalism. He was involved in the Namibian liberation struggle and died in 1970.

Mama Kakarakuze Mungunda: Hero during the resistance of Namibian blacks who in 1959 were being forcibly removed from their neighborhood, known as the Old Location, to the segregated township of Katutura: she set fire to the car of the Mayor of Windhoek in protest and was shot.

There are presently four actual graves at Heroes'Acre: Lt. General (Retired) Jerobeam Dimo Hamaambo (commander in the war for Independence, first chief of Namibian Defense Forces and first to receive a state funeral in Heroes' Acre), freedom fighter Kadanga-Hilukilwa Gertrud "Rikumbu," and heroes of the liberation Comrade David Hosea Merero and Comrade Maxton Joseph Mutongolume.

Modern-day Namibian heroes include Frankie Fredericks, who won the silver medal in the 200 m at the Barcelona Olympics in 1992, and Michelle McLean, Miss Universe 1992.

Unlike many countries, Namibia names streets after living persons, which can become a political embarrassment when circumstances or relationships change. In Windhoek, there is Fidel Castro Street, Robert Mugabe Street, Sam Nujoma Drive, and Nelson Mandela Road. Some streets have been renamed more than once and older maps may show Independence Avenue as Kaiser Wilhelmstrasse, for example.

GENDER RELATIONS

As we have seen, gender relations moved from quasi equality before the arrival of Christianity to restrictions on women's rights instituted by the South Africans. Today in Namibia, women are regaining their status, though they are still paid significantly less than men for similar jobs.

Namibian law provides for legal access to birth control, as well as rights to child support for children. Twenty-five percent of women use modern birth control methods, which has resulted in an average of five children each, lower than for the rest of Africa. A widow's right to family property is not guaranteed—if her husband dies, his parents and siblings may appropriate his property for their own use.

Homosexuality

The gay community in Namibia is small, at least publicly, but becoming more active within the context of several supporting organizations, including the Rainbow Project. As in much of Africa, there is a pervasive tribal attitude of homophobia and some Namibian government ministers have been very outspoken in their condemnation of homosexuality, saying it is un-African and un-Christian. While not as open a society for gays as South Africa, Namibia is becoming more tolerant of sexual difference.

HIV/AIDS

Namibia has one of the highest rates of HIV/AIDS in Africa, which varies by region from 9 to 43 percent. As of 2004, one in five Namibians aged fifteen to forty-nine is HIV positive. The HIV/AIDS prevalence rate is estimated to be 22.3 percent. Statistics show that the Ovambo tribe has the one of the highest rates of AIDS in Africa, while it is rare among the Himbas, who live in isolated villages and usually have only one partner.

Women in Namibia have proved to be at higher risk than men for a variety of reasons:

- Traditionally, women may not refuse sex to their husbands or force them to wear condoms.
- Twelve percent of Namibian women live in polygamous unions, which obviously increases the number of a husband's sexual partners.

- The sexual initiation of young women is often with experienced older men who have had many sexual partners.
- Women face social or family pressure to have children, which places them at risk when they have unprotected sex in order to conceive; there is a high incidence of mother to child transmission during childbirth.
- *Levirate*, the custom in which the brother of a deceased man "inherits" his brother's wife is still practiced by some of Namibia's ethnic groups.
- Many husbands leave their wives in rural areas to seek work in the city, where they engage in sexual liaisons with other women, often transmitting the virus to their wives when they return home.

Some people say that AIDS prevention campaigns are less successful than elsewhere because they are based on assumptions of nonexistent free choice in sexual matters. Other considerations are the fact that sex workers, who are generally living in poverty, accept extra money to allow clients sex without the use of condoms; and that, as some young people report, the churches advise against the use of condoms for religious reasons. As a visitor to the country, it is essential to take precautions to avoid contracting AIDS.

ATTITUDES TOWARD TIME

In a country with excellent weather most of the year, as well as long distances to travel between towns, there is not a sense of urgency regarding time, outside certain business and industrial settings, public transportation, and schools. That is not to say that events don't take place. When something is scheduled, it will almost always happen—just not always exactly at the stated time. You will find that German-Namibians are more concerned with being punctual than many other segments of the population.

PERSONAL SPACE AND PRIVACY

Namibians who live in remote—and particularly tribal—settings, are accustomed to sharing small living quarters with larger groups than those who live in independent houses in cities. This includes a lack of what Western Europeans or Americans would consider essential privacy; however, in these situations, Namibians show respect for others and have ways of allowing others space for personal activities. It should be mentioned that Namibians are not confrontational as a rule and, therefore, do not invade another's personal space in an aggressive manner.

chapter three

BELIEFS, CUSTOMS, & TRADITIONS

CUSTOMS AND RITUALS

Despite the emergence of a modern society, many of the customs and traditions of Namibia's diverse ethnic groups are still celebrated and maintained, especially in the rural areas that make up most of the country. There is really no exact line of demarcation between the *then* and the *now*.

Hunting

For most tribes hunting involved—and still does in some places today, especially in parts of

Bushmanland in the eastern part of Namibia—a system of complicated rituals, many involving requests and prayers to ancestors. In those tribes with kings, hunting was tightly controlled, with some areas or species reserved only for royal hunting. The Uukwambi

(Ovambo) were required to ask the king for permission to hunt, but they were not allowed to kill an eland, whose soft skin was reserved to dress the wife of the king. The Bushmen in particular are known for taking only what they need from nature and never to the point of irreparable destruction.

Though men and women traditionally sought a balance of strength in their relationships, some rituals required the woman to give up a part of her strength to her husband while he was on a hunt. Abstinence from sex the night prior to embarking on a hunt was common; sometimes, if the hunt was for dangerous animals, such as elephant, lion, rhino, buffalo, or hippopotamus, abstinence was extended to two days before the hunt, so that the hunter (or fisherman) could stay "as pure as he was born." While the hunters were out, their wives were required to work quietly, speak in low voices, avoid working with sharp implements (needles or tools), and do no housework. It was necessary to keep the fire burning; otherwise, the hunter's luck would die. In the Topnaar (Nama), the wife of a fisherman was not to visit her neighbors while he was out fishing; otherwise, the fish might swim around, too, making them more difficult to catch. She was not to throw cold water on the fire while her husband was out fishing.

The Kavango are skilled hunters, known for catching crocodiles by using a fishing line baited

with meat and with a wooden board on the other end—if the croc took the bait, he would be compelled to swim with the floating wood. Once he tired, the Kavango made the kill.

There are still animals to hunt in some parts of Namibia; in other remote areas, animals are being reintroduced for cultural and educational reasons (so-called "ritual" hunting, to preserve tribal traditions, for example), as well as for sustainable conservation for tourism and "profane" hunting (meat for the community to eat). Some tribes are eager to reinstate lost traditions not only to restore game, but also to be able to demonstrate their culture to visitors.

Trophy hunting was introduced to Namibia by the Germans, who had their own elaborate set of rituals. After the kill, the hunt guide would cut two small branches from a bush; one branch went into the mouth of the animal, symbolizing its last meal, while

the other was given to the hunter to be placed on his hat. The animal was then placed with its head facing the hunter, who put his own piece of branch on the middle of the body to show ownership. Controlled trophy hunting is still permitted in Namibia, where hunt guides are registered and game conservation is practiced.

There are other rituals associated not only with hunting, but also with certain significant life events, such as when a baby has his first haircut or a new home is built. In today's world, these rituals continue to be practiced, although they have been adapted for those living in the cities.

Water Ceremonies

In the Nyae Nyae Conservancy, a ceremony used to be performed in the old days (and sometimes is today) to pray for water during a drought. The elders would meet and bring seeds, hoes, and other farming equipment. An altar was built and the seeds and equipment gathered under it. A container made from a calabash (gourd) was filled with water and left overnight. The next morning, the whole village gathered. One of the elders would take a mouthful of water and spit it out in all directions. A fresh reed was cut and used as a whistle, while the elders prayed, "Almighty, when you hear this sound, don't think it is a bird calling. It's me, your servant. We are getting burnt down here." After more prayers, the people would then chant, "the rain is coming, the rain is coming."

Storytelling

The *karetsanadi* are folk tales and songs of praise passed down through the generations to perpetuate the memory of the Namas' common history. There are several hundred folktales, some of which have forty variations.

Other Rituals

In Herero culture, the holy fire is lit at dawn and dusk by the oldest man in the village. Then all the men sit together and talk. In the case of illness, death, or impending marriage, the entire family will come to the fire to ask the ancestors for help.

In Ovambo culture, when an elephant died, the tusks were used to make jewelry. (Today, Namibia is not covered by the Convention on International Trade in Endangered Species [CITES] ban on ivory, as elephants are not an endangered species.) Animal skins were used to carry babies; cheetah skins reserved to carry the sons of the king.

BIRTH, DEATH, AND LIFE EVENTS
Death and the Afterlife

In Kaokoland there are places called *ombindi*, where the ancestors carried bodies to their final rest. A stone would be left, and when friends or relatives passed by they added another stone—*ombindi* can still be pointed out today. No hunting was allowed near these spots unless the king approved after consulting the holy fire.

The Kavango believe that the western sky is a bad place; therefore, the dead are buried with their heads facing west.

The Nama bury their dead in an isolated place, away from the village. Rocks cover the grave to keep the spirit of the person from rising again. A black flag is hung at the house of the deceased (in the case of a wedding, also an elaborate event, white flags are hung at the homes of the bride and groom). The funeral is always on Saturday. On Friday, the mourners sing late into the night, facing eastward at dawn to greet the new day and leave the dead behind. On Sunday, the relatives and friends come to comfort the bereaved family.

To the Damara, Heaven is a village where []Gamab is the headman; the elders of this village are thought to be cannibals. To the Damara, this is why only bones are found in an old grave. To ensure that the spirits of the dead do not return, corpses are tied up before burial and rocks are placed on top of the grave. Traditionally, the home of the deceased was abandoned; in today's more practical world, the doorway is closed and a new one made on the other side of the house.

When a German Namibian dies, toasts are drunk to the deceased after the funeral; the Basters will drink only tea and coffee as a sign of respect.

According to bankers in small towns, when an Ovambo man dies, his brothers and family, not including the widow, go to the bank to clean out the account of the deceased.

Because of the arid climate, many local cemeteries in Namibian towns have no grass or trees, and graves are dug into the dirt. Many headstones are painted on stone or wood rather than engraved.

Healing Rituals

Despite the availability of modern medicine in the big cities, many Namibians still visit traditional healers, where the spirits of animals, such as giraffe, eland, and oryx, are invoked to provide guidance for these healers. The San/Bushmen call upon the spirits of their ancestors to aid in healing, often by dancing together.

In some traditional communities, certain rituals were performed in the case of epidemics and can still take place today in very remote areas. The entire community was expected to abstain from all sexual activity, all houses were cleaned, all fires extinguished, and fireplaces cleared. The next morning, a new sacrificial altar was created outside and the king lit the new fire and prayed to god, the ancestors, the "sun of god," the "moon of god," and the "stars of god." Afterward, young boys were sent to hunt for small birds and animals and young women pounded millet. The meat and millet were cooked close to the sacrificial altar; only the old people ate some of the food. The rest of the cooked millet was made into small balls, which were attached to sticks. The king then led the whole community on a westward march, where they threw the sticks toward the setting sun (West is the direction of death) and prayed for the sickness to die. Then they all returned home, taking a spark from the fire to restart their own hearth fires.

In Ovambo culture, traditional healers used the horns of springbok and impala to cure mad people. They believed that the sound coming from soft blowing into the horn would find its way into the brain of a mentally handicapped person and reorganize it into normal function.

Rites of Passage

In the San/Bushman culture, wildlife is often used in rituals and an entranced person will seem to take the form of an animal. In a young women's initiation ceremony, she is chased around the menstrual hut by a man dressed as an eland. In Ovambo culture, an initiation ceremony called Ohango celebrated this rite of passage.

Just before puberty, every Himba boy and girl has four lower incisors removed and "given back" to their place of birth. It is socially unacceptable not to remove these teeth.

At puberty, a Himba boy is circumcised. The girl must leave the village at her first menses until she goes through a ritual for spiritual protection, conducted by the other women in a special enclosure. She will be given gifts and new clothes.

Marriage

In Ovamboland, a wedding lasts from
Thursday to Sunday, when the bride is
"handed over." The traditional *lobola*

was a gift of cattle from the groom to the bride's
family, as mentioned earlier, to show his wealth;
today it is informally considered a "purchase" and
involves an elaborate wedding. Some Ovambos in
remote areas are still polygamous, as are some
Hereros, though the practice is officially illegal.

A Himba woman moves to her husband's new
family after she marries and begins to dress like a
married woman, wearing particular jewelry and
arranging her hair in a topknot. Herero women
begin to wear the traditional Victorian dresses
and headpieces after marriage.

MANNERS
Greetings

A Herero child is greeted by rubbing sand behind
its neck. When Hereros meet people they haven't
seen in a long time or people they don't know,
they gather in a circle and pass a jug of water
from the oldest to the youngest person. Each
takes a mouthful and spits out three small
amounts before passing the jug to the next oldest.
Once this has been done by everyone, the group
begins to greet and kiss.

Ovambos shake hands in a particular way
shared by other Africans. While shaking the hand

of the other person with their right hand, an Ovambo places his or her left hand under the right arm. If it is an important person being greeted, they will place the left hand on their heart. There can be a very long greeting procedure, with many handshakes.

Showing Respect

Hereros show respect for their elders by waiting to be greeted first. Younger people have no right to talk to their elders first.

Caprivians show respect to their elders by approaching them on their knees, expecting a kiss on the palm in return. Elderly people are served food and drink by younger people on their knees. In the case of the chief, they crawl to greet him. Caprivians clap as a sign of respect.

Afrikaners wait for the person of older or higher status to greet them first. It is a sign of respect to wait to be approached by the senior person.

Eating

Sometimes, particularly in traditional settings, Ovambos eat with their hands, as do some other tribes.

HOLIDAYS AND CELEBRATIONS

Namibians love a party and a public holiday is an excuse to have one. Big outdoor events are well attended, especially Independence celebrations,

PUBLIC HOLIDAYS IN NAMIBIA

January 1 New Year's Day

March 21 Independence Day

March/April Good Friday and Easter Monday

May 1 Workers' Day

May 4 Cassinga Day (commemorating the lives of several hundred Namibians shot by the South Africa Defense Forces in 1978)

May Ascension Day

May 25 Africa Day (commemorating the founding of the Organization of African Unity)

August 26 Heroes Day (to remember the beginning of SWAPO's armed struggle in 1966 and all those killed in the name of Namibian independence)

December 10 International Human Rights Day (to remember the day in 1959 when residents of the Old Location, the black township, were forcibly removed by the South African *apartheid* regime to Katutura, where many families still live today)

December 25 Christmas (celebrated December 24 by the German community)

December 26 Family Day, called Boxing Day in England, is a day devoted to the family

and often there are parties with families or friends on holidays. A long weekend will see many Namibians hit the road to camp or stay in a bungalow in one of the many national parks, where they will bring out the charcoal for a *braaivleis*.

OTHER CELEBRATIONS AND MEMORIALS

Often ethnic groups will wear traditional costume and serve traditional foods at these events.

End of April/early May Windhoek Karneval, with its Prinzenball, German celebration

May 8–9 Rehoboth Basters mark the ambush of the Basters by the Germans in 1915, when they were hiding to keep from fighting for the Germans in the First World War.

Weekend closest to June 11 Mbanderu Herero (Green Flag) Day at Okahandja

August/September Kuste Karneval (Coast Carnival) in Swakopmund

Weekend closest to August 26 Maherero (Red Flag) Day in Okahandja

October Oktoberfest in Windhoek

Weekend closest to October 10 White Flag Herero Day in Omaruru; ovoryone wears black and white

November Damara Day at Okambahe

chapter four

MEETING NAMIBIANS

Though it is a small population, Namibian society is so diverse that invariably one comes in contact with people from other cultures. What they all share is a commitment to the "new" independent Namibia and the idea of national reconciliation. In the past, the general German and South African government policy was to keep various tribes apart from one another in order to control them better. Since Independence, many more biracial or bicultural friendships have developed, as people get to know others from outside their traditional social or familial group.

Namibians, like people everywhere, make friends in a variety of ways. In remote areas, the extended family often includes the whole village; cousins are considered sisters and brothers. Today, even further afield, various ethnic groups come into contact with people from other cultures: work colleagues, tourists, international aid workers, and others. For city dwellers, in addition to family there are lifelong friendships with childhood friends and friends from boarding school, university, or church. New friendships

develop in adulthood as they meet people with
common interests, work together, or enlarge their
circle through marriage or children.

FORGING FRIENDSHIPS

When Namibian Wildlife Resorts, the
hospitality arm of the Ministry of Environment
and Tourism, built the new Sossus Dune Lodge
within the park at Sossusvlei, it was deliberately
decided to staff the project with young
Namibians from every tribe and ethnic group.
Because Namibia is so big, many of the new
staffers had never met members of tribes from
other parts of the country.

An Ovambo server said that she had enjoyed
meeting a Bushman for the first time, and that
she had become great friends with him, while a
Herero bartender remarked how interesting it
was to work with so many different kinds of
people within his own country. The manager,
an Afrikaner, noted that she and her employees
use English as the common language, because
many of them do not speak the tribal languages
of their coworkers. The employees in this
remote area work together for three months,
meeting guests from all over the world, before
taking a one-month break. In their time
together, they form strong bonds and,
potentially, lifelong friendships.

As everywhere in the world, the qualities valued by Namibians in their friends include loyalty, honesty, commitment to family, and shared interests; they appreciate being able to rely on each other, laugh together, and share traditions.

The introduction of English as the official language after Independence in 1990 has changed the texture of cross-cultural relationships. After more than fifteen years, English is now the glue that holds together a society where the various segments do not otherwise have a common tongue. Today, friendships across racial and tribal divides are becoming more common.

COUPLES ACROSS RACE AND CULTURE

Biracial and bicultural couples are becoming more common in Namibia. There have always been segments of society that have been biracial, such as Coloreds and Rehoboth Basters, or bicultural —Afrikaans–German, or Herero–Ovambo, for example. A number of high-ranking officials in the Namibian government are part of biracial or bicultural couples, which is a public example of the acceptability of such unions.

The so-called *petty apartheid* laws (governing interracial marriage, separate neighborhoods, and public facilities) were repealed in Namibia in 1978, long before they were in South Africa, but social and business segregation continued unofficially for many years. In addition, *grand apartheid*, which affected voting and other civil rights, continued until just before Independence. Almost two decades after Independence, blacks and whites live and work together all over Namibia, though some neighborhoods and areas of the country continue to be predominantly one race or tribe. As mentioned above, the introduction of English as the official language has done much to bring various elements of society together and has increased the number of couples who come from different backgrounds, races, or cultures.

GETTING TO KNOW NAMIBIANS

For an outsider, an open and friendly attitude is the key to connecting with Namibians. Certainly, speaking English increases the opportunities to talk to young people from different tribes who have learned it at school, while Afrikaans can also be useful.

Namibians are generally very friendly and outgoing and most want to meet foreigners. Sometimes blacks are more willing to speak to strangers than whites, both because theirs is a culture of community and because Namibian young people want to know more about the world beyond their borders. This is not to say that whites are unfriendly, but that culturally they have a more defined sense of personal space. Young people of all races in Namibia are likely to be more open to new acquaintances than their elders. A good opening gambit, particularly with the opposite sex, is to ask polite questions about their country: Is Etosha National Park the best place to see animals? Where is the best informal eatery in Windhoek? Where can you find a good place to eat or drink in Katutura? Where are the best places to hear music? Which is the best place to buy souvenirs or crafts? If there is one thing Namibians like to talk about it, it is their extraordinary country, and everyone has an opinion on the most exciting place to go.

As we have seen, Namibians from all backgrounds share a concern for nature and the environment, and this is a great topic of conversation. Avoid talking politics, religion, or hunting, as you will encounter mixed views on certain issues. These subjects are best left for later. Rain and when it's coming is a safe topic, as are their last safari/camping adventure, when they are traveling and where, good new restaurants, suggestions on which South African wines to try, and the like. You can also ask a black person which tribe they are from and about their traditions and culture—remember that no tradition is exactly the same in every place.

ATTITUDES TOWARD FOREIGNERS
Namibians live in such a multicultural society that meeting someone "different" is easier for them than it might be for others. For the most part, they are eager to meet people from elsewhere and have many

questions to ask about other places and lifestyles. Many Namibians have traveled abroad to study, attend trade fairs, and so on, and have experience of other countries.

MEETING AND GREETING

In an informal context, the "African Handshake" is used between blacks and whites and blacks and blacks. Shake hands and, without letting go, slip your hand around the other person's thumb; then go back to the traditional handshake. Whites do not use this handshake with other whites.

With good friends of the opposite sex, men kiss women on one cheek. Men greet close male friends with a handshake or a hug. In greeting men in a business setting, women either nod or shake hands in the European way.

TIME IN A SOCIAL SETTING

In a country as multicultural as Namibia, there are differing ideas about time. If you are invited to a German or Afrikaans home for a social event, you should arrive at the time stated. If it is the home of an Ovambo, Herero, or other member of an indigenous tribe, you may come a bit late without seeming rude. If you are invited to the official residence of someone in government or diplomacy, you should arrive on time, and bring your passport or other identification documents in case there are guards checking the invitation list at the door. Meeting friends at a restaurant or bar calls for arriving no more than ten minutes late without calling, unless you have set a very flexible schedule. Don't use traffic as an excuse if you're late, as there isn't that much. You could say a kudu blocked the road if you're in the bush; otherwise, make an effort to arrive on time.

On the other hand, when you invite guests, you may expect Germans and Afrikaners to be prompt, while others may be late (half an hour) to very late (more than an hour). If the guest of honor is very late, you must wait for him or her, or call to be certain they are coming. It's okay to serve drinks and snacks while you are waiting. If the event is casual, such as a *braai*, you may start to eat the main course at a certain point; if it is a seated dinner, then you will have to make certain that your tardy guest is indeed on the way and, if so, wait for him/her before sitting down to eat.

Lunch is usually around 12:30 for 1:00 p.m. (arrive between 12:30 and 1:00 p.m., with the expectation of going to table at 1:00); dinner is often 7:30 for 8:00 p.m. or later. Casual evenings can go on until very late, while most business dinners will finish at a reasonable hour, especially on weekday evenings. If you are attending a formal or diplomatic dinner, it is rude to leave before the guest of honor. (If you are the guest of honor and see everyone around you yawning, you need to say good night and let them all go home.)

INVITATIONS HOME

Always bring a gift for the host(ess) when invited to a private home. Flowers (it is very nice to send them ahead of time), wine, a small bowl for serving nuts, or some small item from your home country is appreciated. Nothing personal should be given.

On arrival, as well as before departing, you should go around the room to greet or meet and shake hands with everyone. Once you know someone well, it is common for men and women to kiss on both cheeks as well as for two women to kiss on both cheeks. Handshakes range from the subdued European manner to the more complicated and hearty African style. Generally, the host or hostess will make the introductions.

For the most part, table manners are European, with fork held in the left hand and not switched to the right, American-style. Both hands are generally kept in view. Wine or beer may be served and there is usually at least a word of "cheers" before everyone drinks. Wait for everyone to be served before you eat, unless you are at a *braai* or buffet meal. Some Africans traditionally eat with their hands when in their home village and, on occasion at a formal dinner, you might see someone pick up a bone to savor the last bits. If this bothers you, remember you are in a country where table manners come in an infinite variety. Refrain from smoking at table between courses, even if ashtrays have been provided, unless your host lights up.

When visiting a Namibian family, especially in remote areas, expect extended greetings and handshakes. If food and drink is offered, it is polite to accept.

If you are invited to a ladies' coffee or tea party in the home of an older Namibian, particularly an Afrikaner, don't be surprised if the event takes place with everyone seated around the dining room table, rather than in the living room. Also, when there is a mixed group, the men may stay in the living room to talk, while the women will be led by the hostess to the dining room.

Coffee and Diplomacy

On one occasion, an important older Namibian and his wife invited a group of ambassadors and their spouses for coffee to meet a visiting VIP. When everyone had arrived, the wife stood up and invited all the ladies to join her for coffee in the dining room while the diplomats talked, forgetting that one of the ambassadors was a woman. The ambassador in question joined the other women, took two polite sips of her coffee, and then stood up, saying, "Thank you. I'll now join my colleagues, if you don't mind."

APPROPRIATE DRESS

Traditional tribal or national dress is always acceptable for both hosts and guests and adds much to any social occasion. Colorful African dresses and headpieces, Indian saris, Indonesian batik shirts, and other styles of dress can be seen often on the streets and at events in Namibia. The distinctive Herero women's traditional Victorian-style dress described earlier, with its headpiece tied to resemble cow horns, is perhaps the most recognized on the streets of Namibian towns, while further north there may be Himba women in traditional attire (topless, with cowhide skirts) shopping in the grocery stores.

For the visitor, the primary consideration is the heat. Whether casual, smart casual, or formal, garments made from natural fabrics will be the most comfortable and appropriate, especially if events are held outside. Hats to block the sun, sunglasses, and sun block are a must. Open shoes are appropriate almost anywhere, though men should avoid them on business occasions.

Young people the world over may favor miniskirts, cropped tops, and very low-slung jeans, but visitors to Namibia should dress a bit more conservatively, though casually. Bare arms are all right, but bare cleavage is a bit too much.

A *braaivleis* is a very informal event, usually on the patio or in the garden. Dress is very casual and long shorts and jeans are acceptable. Tennis shoes, flip-flops, or sandals are fine.

A Word to the Wise
Locals do wear African prints, which depict politicians, flowers, or geometric symbols, but Namibians don't often wear garments with animal patterns, such as leopard skin or zebra stripes. People who wear such clothes stand out as tourists. Another thing: although you may have purchased new clothes to wear on safari, you will look more of an insider if you wash them a few times before coming to Namibia. The safari suit hasn't been seen around in a while.

A dinner party usually demands "smart casual" attire. This means nicer sportswear, worn with jewelry if you wish, not jeans or shorts. Namibian women tend to be very smart dressers, wearing well-cut natural fabrics, often with fine jewelry mixed with local artisanal pieces. A woman might go to a dinner party in summer in a linen sundress or dressier pants and shirt, while a man would wear slacks and a sports shirt. Collared knit golf shirts, but not T-shirts, work in this setting. Wintertime, when the evenings are cold, calls for blazers, sweaters, shawls and woolen skirts, woolen or khaki-type slacks, and the like. Loafers, high or low heels, but not tennis shoes or flip-flops, are acceptable footwear.

A formal event, such as stipulated on a wedding invitation, would call for suit and tie (unless it says black tie, in which case a tuxedo is necessary) for men, and cocktail or long dress for women. Many Namibian women own fur coats made from the skin of the karakul lamb and these can be worn to formal events or dinner parties.

When going out into the bush, whether camping or visiting a lodge, subdued colors are more acceptable than bright ones, as they are less likely to disturb the animals. During a game drive, khaki pants or shorts, or jeans, are good, along with shirt or T-shirt. Long sleeves are preferable on hot days because of the sun; at the very least wear sun block and a hat. Evenings at a lodge are casual; sometimes evenings are chilly, so a cotton sweater, windbreaker, or quilted vest is good to have.

For clubbing, casual dress is the norm, though young women tend to dress up a bit. Less conservative is okay, but stay away from blatant sexuality. Women might wear high-heeled sandals with their jeans or shorter skirts to go out in the evening.

Business dress is the same as in Europe or the USA, at least for the first meeting—suit and tie for men, suit or dress or pantsuit for women. Your host may not be dressed as formally, but you should look polished and professional. Going to professional or other meetings, such as the Rotary Club, requires a jacket and tie. In both instances, it may be possible to remove the jacket or tie after you arrive.

DATING AND MAKING FRIENDS

Making a possible date or making friends in Namibia is easier if you have an introduction; if you don't, be open, but nonaggressive. Clubs are often the places where younger visitors meet young Namibians. Other opportunities come on the road, at lodges, hotels, and small restaurants in little towns. Namibians, black and white, are ready to answer questions about their town, their country, local activities, and the like. Asking the location of the nearest Internet café may result in a personal escort to the place; another good

subject is cell phone reception and where to buy top-ups or recharge.

Don't confuse dress style (the topless Himba women, as discussed earlier) with lack of conservative values, or cultural misunderstandings can arise. Namibians are more conservative than not, and it is wise to take relationships slowly. While women in various tribes may be culturally trained not to say no to sexual advances from men in their own sphere, this does not mean they are open to advances from foreigners. Of course, safe sex is a necessity.

Public displays of affection between spouses or lovers are not considered appropriate, especially in rural areas, but hugging is common among friends.

chapter five

THE NAMIBIANS AT HOME

Over the past several decades, the traditional way of life in parts of Namibia has changed and there are now more modern suburbs outside the cities, similar to those in the USA and Europe, than in the past. There are still many villages with traditional huts in rural areas, but more and more are being replaced with cement-block houses with tin roofs or similar structures.

THE FAMILY

Family life is as varied as Namibia's diverse population. Homes range from contemporary mansions with all the modern conveniences, to round huts with no water and electricity. In between are remote farmhouses, beachside condominiums, square concrete houses, and residences made from discarded materials, such as oil drums, sheets of tin, and cans. About one-third of houses have electricity and indoor plumbing. In many families, particularly tribal groups living in remote areas, multiple generations share a home; the average household has five to seven members.

Those traditional villages that do still exist are well organized and often enclosed. A Himba village, for example, consists of round huts placed near the wooden perimeter fence, with the center space left open for maintaining the holy fire, work (such as weaving baskets or making jewelry), and socializing. This concept holds true for other tribes, although the structure may be shaped differently.

What all these families have in common is a concern for their children and a hope for a better future. Many children of black families are breast-fed and carried tied to their mother's backs until they are around two years old. Most of them sleep with their mothers and children share beds, or a bedroom if there is enough space.

Parents and other family members often share child-rearing responsibilities and children may live with relatives other than their parents if they need to be closer to their school or if their parents are working elsewhere.

Families of Western European or Afrikaner origin share a desire for more privacy, valuing personal space. Often, they have hired help for the housework and children.

There is a problem of domestic violence in many segments of Namibian society, both black and white. More than one-fifth of violent crimes occur within domestic relationships. Poverty, unemployment, the HIV/AIDs epidemic, and gender issues contribute to the problem. In response, the government has established refuges for abused women and children in Windhoek and in Oshakati in the north.

EDUCATION

The education policy of Namibia was completely revamped after Independence in 1990 in an effort to move away from the *apartheid* system. English is the language of instruction from grade 5 on, while the fourteen local languages are used in early grades. More than 95 percent of children attend at least primary school, though some in remote areas are kept away to tend to the livestock. Street children, who have been orphaned by AIDS, often do not go to school. In rural areas, children often walk miles to school, with a few having access to a bicycle or donkey. (See Chapter 7, Transport.)

Education is compulsory and basically free for ten years between the ages of six and sixteen, though parents are expected to pay for some books and uniform. Primary education is for seven years, and secondary school lasts for five years. Approximately 50 percent of students continue past grade 10, at age sixteen. Strategies outlined in Vision 2030, the government's education project, include increasing vocational training centers, improving teaching of math, science, and technology, and encouraging the development of entrepreneurial skills.

Children who live far from schools, whether black or white, often spend the weekdays in hostels attached to their school, which may be public or private. There are fee-paying private schools in Namibia, ranging from the German and the American schools to religious schools, such as St. Paul's and St. George's. Some Namibians, if they can afford to, send their children to private boarding schools in South Africa or Europe.

Private schools often offer scholarships to students who cannot afford to pay; the fact that a student has received a scholarship is usually a matter between the school and the student and is not public knowledge.

University education is provided by the University of Namibia, located in Windhoek, which offers degrees from the colleges of Agriculture and Natural Resources, Economics and Management, Science Education, Humanities and Social Science, Law, Medical and Health Science, and Science. The University of Namibia is the only institution to offer a doctorate in the study of the Nama language.

In addition, there is the Polytechnic of Namibia, a university of technology located in Windhoek. It comprises five academic schools: the Schools of Engineering Information Technology, Business and Management, Natural Resources and Tourism, and Communication. The polytechnic offers certificates, national diplomas, and bachelor's and master's degrees.

Military Service
Service in the Namibian Defense Force (Army, Navy, Air Wing) is voluntary, with a minimum age of eighteen.

DAILY LIFE

In rural areas, daily life revolves around domestic animals (cattle or goats), obtaining water and firewood, cooking or preparing food, and household chores. Men in seminomadic tribes may herd cattle or goats in remote areas, while the women gather firewood or water. Himba women often make a kind of yogurt from the milk of the tribe's cattle, while other tribal women harvest millet or other crops. With the emergence of deforestation as a critical problem in parts of the country, what used to be an hour's work collecting firewood has, in some areas, become an all-day pursuit. Going to the well to collect water in rural Namibia can be an opportunity to meet and greet friends, lessening the tedium of this daily chore. On both communal and

commercial farms, every member of the family has responsibility for some portion of running the property.

In Namibia's small towns, daily life revolves around the outdoor market, the school, and domestic chores. There are retail establishments and banks to work in, as well as roadside stands along the highway, where handmade items can be sold. Church is important for social life, as well as religious enrichment.

Life in the bigger cities is more varied. There are businesses to run, schoolchildren to drop off, banks and other offices to staff. Since school starts as early as 7:00 a.m., households get up early during the week. The larger towns offer many recreational activities, which take up the leisure time of men, women, and children: golf, horseback riding, ballet lessons, choirs, gym, and so on.

MEDICAL CARE

Medical care in Namibia is excellent in the towns, but more scarce in remote areas. The doctor/patient ratio is one doctor per 7,000 people, one of the best in Africa. All major towns have state-run hospitals and there are well-equipped clinics that service smaller towns and villages.

SUMMER VACATIONS

Summer vacations are generally taken in December and January, during the school holidays. The most popular place to spend the holidays is in Swakopmund or other nearby communities along the Atlantic coast. Beaches, restaurants, and hotels are full of vacationers, including the Namibian president, whose summer residence is in Swakopmund. Those who can afford it have vacation homes in that area, while others rent houses for up to two months. The Namibian Wildlife Resorts arm of the Ministry of Environment and Tourism has facilities to rent near the beach in Swakopmund; there is accommodation in or near Swakopmund ranging from the pension or bed and breakfast level to four-star resorts.

chapter six

TIME OUT

Namibians are happiest when they are out of doors, and think nothing of driving a thousand miles in a day, or camping in the most remote

areas on earth. People of all races like to entertain, especially with a *braaivleis* (literally, grilled meat) at home or at a campsite. An Afrikaner tradition that has spread across the country, the *braaivleis*, or *braai*, is most typically a social or family event involving cooking meat over an outdoor fire.

Rural Namibians, who spend much of their time doing farmwork, do not have official paid time off and cannot leave their livestock to go on vacation. Still, they enjoy the time they do have to the fullest.

For a visitor, the best way to join in with Namibians is eating and drinking, especially outdoors. Namibians are generous hosts and are happy to throw another kudu steak on the fire or pop open a beer for a stranger.

Tourists traveling in Namibia will find picnic tables every six or seven miles along major roads, often with grills for barbecuing. All national parks have *braaivleis* facilities for cookouts and picnics. Because the country is so dry, it is important to observe fire safety rules when lighting outdoor fires.

EATING AND DRINKING
Traditional Foods

Namibia's food is very varied and reflects its multicultural society. Meat includes homegrown cattle, which is primarily grass fed and delicious. In addition, there are lamb and goat, and wild game such as springbok, kudu, eland, or oryx (gemsbok) cut into steaks or made into savory sausages called *boerewors*. Venison is tasty in a *potjiekos*, a spicy stew cooked in a three-legged iron pot over an open fire. Crocodile, warthog, impala, ostrich, or zebra may also be on offer. Goat heads cooked on an open fire are a favorite of

many Namibians, who call them "smileys" because, when cooked, the head seems to be grinning.

Maize porridge, or *mieliepap*, made from white maize meal is a staple African food in both cities and remote areas. It can be eaten at any meal;

Afrikaans-style it is often served with tomato sauce or meat juices to accompany game grilled outside on the *braai*. A close relative is *mahangu* (pearl millet, which has been grown in Africa for centuries), a staple food of many families in the north. The grains are stored either in granaries or pounded to make *oshifima*. Proper eating of *oshifima* requires a bit of fortitude, as earth from anthills is used in harvesting and threshing the grain and there may be sand and small stones left behind. It is impolite to remove the stones from your mouth; rather, the *oshifima* is softened with the tongue and everything is swallowed together.

Oshifima is served with chicken, meat, or *edingue*, a sauce made from dried meat, along with *ekaka*, wild spicy spinach that grows in the *mahangu* fields.

Other traditional delicacies include the mopane worm (*omaungu*), a colorful caterpillar named after the mopane tree leaves on which they feed. Mopane worms are prepared by squeezing out the insides, drying them in the sun, and then frying them, often with tomatoes, onion, and chilies. Mopanes are popular as snacks and are sold wrapped in newspaper around the country. In Windhoek, they are available at the Katutura outdoor market.

With its long Atlantic coast, Namibia offers visitors a wonderful array of fresh seafood. Oyster lovers will find some of the best in the world, at a price as palatable as the oysters. Try both Lüderitz and Swakopmund oysters to compare the taste—both are excellent. Succulent grilled crayfish are also plentiful, along with other shellfish, hake, steenbras, and kabeljou that come directly out of the Atlantic Ocean off Namibia's coast.

Namibia's German heritage remains in the breads, pastries, *Schnitzels, Sauerkraut, Spatzle* noodles, and local beer. Enticing German desserts are found in bakeries in the smallest towns, including *Schwarzwalderkirschtorte, Apfelstrudel,* and *Sachertorte.*

Seasonal specialties not to be missed are the huge *omajowa* (Herero, mushrooms), which appear like magic at the base of termite hills after February rainstorms; the *nabba* (Nama, Kalahari truffles), found in the sandy regions of the east after rare May and June rains; and fresh Swakopmund asparagus, all on the menu at many restaurants.

Other special dishes include appetizers made from smoked venison, as well as wild game pâtés. *Biltong* (dried meat) is a staple across every section of Namibian culture. The pumpkin fritters and guava fruit juice are addictive, as is non-caffeinated *rooibos* tea, an old Bushman infusion made from a wild bush, which today is sold all over the world. An ostrich egg omelet can be a treat but is best shared—as one ostrich egg equals twenty-four hen eggs.

Drink

South Africa's most important contribution to Namibian cuisine after the *braai* is the wine. Red, white, rosé, and sparkling wines from South Africa are celebrated throughout the world and are available all over Namibia. In addition, there are now several Namibian wines worth trying.

Local Namibian beer is excellent and brewed in the German style. Another favorite nonalcoholic drink is rock shandy, made with lemonade, soda water, and Angostura bitters; shandys can also be made with beer.

Adventuresome souls will try the home brewed beer (accounting for 67 percent of all alcohol consumed in Namibia) sold at the outdoor market in Katutura. The beer is usually made by mixing sorghum grain, water, and sugar in a clay pot, fermented for a few days, then strained through burlap and returned to the pot. Beer and ice cream can be made from the *omauni* (also called *manguni*) fruit, which has a delicate, fresh taste.

FOOD TERMS

Aardappel bollas: deep-fried balls of mashed potato, flour, egg, and vanilla, dipped in almond flakes (Afrikaans)

Beskuit: a biscuit, or cookie, like an English rusk (Afrikaans)

Bienenstich: a bee-sting cake, served by Café Anton in Swakopmund (German)

Biltong: strips of meat, dried and cured in the sun (Afrikaans)

Bobotie: spicy mutton or beef mince topped with egg and milk custard, baked in the oven, and served with yellow raisin rice (Cape Malay)

Boerewors: highly spiced sausage of mixed pork, beef, and fat (Afrikaans)

Braaivleis: South African barbecue

Brandewyn and coke: brandy and Coke, often called the "Afrikaner's drink"

Brötchen: a roll, the major sandwich ingredient in Namibia (German)

Droewors: dried sausage (Afrikaans)

Eisbein: pork knuckle (German)

Kerrie: curry (Afrikaans)

Koeksisters: a syrupy dessert, a finger food made with batter (Afrikaans)

Mahungu: pearl millet (Ovambo)

Mealie-meal: maize meal served with a relish of tomato, onion, and herb sauce at a *braaivleis*

Melktert: a sweet milk tart (Afrikaans)

Mieliepap: maize meal

Omaere: a sour milk dish (Herero)

Omahango: fruit used to make beer or nonalcoholic drink (Ovambo)

Omauni (Oshiwambo) or *manguni* (Lukavango): an orange-colored fruit about the size of a grapefruit, with a hard skin; inside are two light brown lobes, used to make ice cream or drinks, or a body lotion that stays usable for a few years.

Pannekoek: pancake (Afrikaans)

Potjiekos: A stew with a meat base simmered for hours in a three-legged iron pot (a *potjie*; Namibia's indigenous people use this kind of pot to cook a similar dish) (Afrikaans)

Potjie: turned upside down, with its three legs in the air, the *potjie* can be used over an open fire to cook meat joints (Afrikaans)

Rock shandy: a mix of lemonade, bitters, and soda water

Rohhac: raw meat (German)

Rys: rice (Afrikaans)

Schwarzwalderkirschtorte: Black Forest cake (German)

Sosatie: a kebab with mutton and fat marinated in onions, curry spices, and dried apricots (Afrikaans/Cape Malay)

Souskluitjies: a custard dumpling with sauce (Afrikaans)

Vleis: meat (Afrikaans)

SUPERMARKETS

Take time to wander the aisles of a Namibian supermarket to get an idea of the country's multicultural cuisine. Even the small markets in remote areas have interesting choices. There are curries and spices that reflect the Cape Malay and Indian cultures, as well as mealie-meal (cornmeal), locally raised meats, and a variety of biltong. The salt and pepper mix in the spice department is great for cooking and camping. Stock up on *rooibos* tea and boxed tropical juices.

DINING OUT

In the larger cities, there are ethnic restaurants—African, Italian, Indian, German, Portuguese, Chinese—where you will see locals, as well as tourists from around the world. In small towns, try the hotel restaurants for mostly Afrikaans or German menus.

In Windhoek, Gathemann's is the best place for seasonal specialties and wild game. Katutura Market has fried mopane worms and open-air grills where fresh meat is cooked. Sardinia Pizzeria and Joe's Beer House are good for casual dining. At Leo's at the Castle, at the Heinitzburg Castle, the food and sunset view make a spectacular combination.

In Swakopmund, The Tug is directly on the beach and offers great seafood. Café Anton at the Schweitzerhof Hotel bakes delectable pastries. The Grapevine offers wine and good food, and the Brauhaus Arcade in the center of town has a good German pub.

GAMBLING AND NIGHTLIFE

Casinos are legal in Namibia and there are several hotels and resorts that offer both slot machines and table games. Among them are the Windhoek Country Club Resort, the Kalahari Sands Hotel, and the Swakopmund Hotel & Entertainment Centre, sited in a restored historic train station. There are also small local casinos, which cater to less affluent gamblers.

There are a number of clubs where live popular music can be heard, most of them in Windhoek and its suburbs. Aphrodisiac features live Namibian music, El Cubano is popular with young people, and Blue Note is the place for late-night action.

DRINKING, SMOKING, AND DRUG USE

Namibians drink and smoke in higher numbers than most Europeans or Americans. Forty-five percent of Namibians were smokers in 2000; alcohol abuse is a major problem across all sectors of society, resulting in increasing road accidents and domestic crimes. Driving while under the influence of alcohol is illegal; the legal limit is 0.05 percent.

Dagga (*cannabis sativa*, or marijuana) use is common in some areas, though illegal. A recently proposed law, which set penalties as high as twenty years for a first offense, was not passed. Current Namibian law is a holdover from the South African administration; drug users should beware.

STREET BEGGARS

Street beggars are everywhere in Namibia and, depending upon your point of view, you may want to give them a small coin or two. Those who offer to watch cars in a parking lot have evolved from beggars into businessmen and are usually registered if they are working in Windhoek—they expect only a small payment for their "guard services." In other towns, invariably there will be someone, usually a young man, who will offer to watch the car and possibly sell a wood carving. It is usually worth giving them a very small payment for guard duty, but not necessary to buy anything.

SHOPPING FOR PLEASURE
Street Vendors

Street vendors selling locally made handicrafts can be found in most Namibian towns and cities. Negotiation is expected, but remember that these people make a very modest living selling their work. Beware, however, as there are now people on the streets selling items made in China or other African countries. Open-air markets in towns such as Okahandja or on remote roadways can be good places to find local handicrafts made by the people who are selling them.

Craft Centers

Emporia such as the Namibian Craft Center or Penduka in Windhoek, or others in towns around the country, are excellent places to find items made by local artisans from all over Namibia. Generally, there is little or no negotiation at craft centers.

Traditional products sold at Craft Centers run the gamut from jewelry to rugs and are sourced from the local area. The craft centers in Windhoek bring in handmade products from around the country.

Artisanal/Handmade Crafts

Various Namibian groups are known for particular handicrafts made from beads, seeds, PVC, wood, and other items. The makalani palm nut, called "vegetable ivory," is used to make small, intricate carvings. Carvers can quickly personalize them and they make wonderful key rings or ornaments. Handwoven rugs made from karakul sheep wool are a Namibian tradition. They can be purchased ready-made or custom designed.

Crafts are made from locally available materials and represent an important source of income, particularly for women who work from home in remote areas. Many items are of functional design, such as baskets used in everyday life, which have become collector's items. There are baskets made by Ovambo, Kavango, and Caprivi women used for winnowing grain; they are usually made from the leaves of the makalani palm in shades of brown, purple, and yellow, colors which are obtained by boiling the leaves with bark and roots from various shrubs.

Pottery made by the Ndilimani Pottery Group can be purchased at the Tulongeni Craft Market in Omuthiya, while quilts from the Ekwatho quilt project are sold in the Katutura area of Windhoek. Omaruru pottery is sold in Omaruru and in Windhoek at the Craft Center.

Wood carvings made by men and women are sold in Okahandja at the Namibia Mbangura wood-carvers outdoor market.

Baskets made by Himba women to store milk and fat usually have a narrow neck or mouth and a leather handle for hanging in the *ondiowo* (dwelling). Bowl-shaped baskets are used for sifting grass seeds from ants' nests; Himba women also design bracelets and belts from PVC pipe, which are etched with designs and rubbed with ochre.

Crafts produced by Bushmen/San are marketed by the Omeheke San Trust; G!hunku Crafts market in Tsumkwe also sells Bushman crafts, which include ostrich-shell beads, porcupine quills, nuts, roots, and berries; the ostrich-shell beads are made using a hand bow to drill the central hole and a stone to shape and smooth the edges. There are also beaded antelope skin bags for collecting wild berries or carrying tobacco.

Nama crafts include sewing and embroidery, as well as the *kaross*, a rug or blanket made from skins, often springbok, sewn together. Formerly worn by Khoisan people, today they are used as rugs or bedcovers. These blankets can be purchased from displays on fences along the B1 highway. Nama embroidery can be purchased in various craft centers around the country.

Gemstones and Fine Jewelry
There are many European-trained jewelers and artist-designers who make fine pieces from Namibian diamonds or semiprecious stones, such as tourmalines, amethyst, topaz, lapis lazuli, and many others. Their shops and studios are primarily in Windhoek or Swakopmund.

Traditional Jewelry
Rock paintings, such as the White Lady at the Brandberg Mountain, show that decorative headdresses, bracelets, and belts were worn in Namibia thousands of years ago. Today, the

jewelry worn by Himba women often denotes whether they are married or single—in particular a large white shell worn as a necklace, called the *ohumba,* which is also worn by Ovambo and Herero women.

Ekipas are ornamental buttons made of ivory or bone worn by Ovambo women as status symbols in times past. Uniquely Namibian and southern Angolan, antique *ekipas* are collector's items; today new *ekipas* are being made from ivory, approved by CITES as preservation of a time-honored craft, and sold legally.

Animal Hides

Fashion items made from Namibian ostrich, zebra, and other exotic skins are available in shops around the country and are usually of very high quality. It is illegal to sell skins from endangered species.

Clothing

There are shops selling casual items, such as caps and T-shirts imprinted with Namibian themes, as well as designer jackets and vests made from high quality animal skins. There are safari shops in most cities, which sell bush clothing, seal or kudu leather shoes, hats, belts, and so on.

A joint Namibian-Finnish project, the Pambili Association, makes and exports Namibian design projects to Scandinavian markets. Garments are made from wild silk, cotton, and linen woven by Ibenstein Textiles at Dordabis; felt slippers and

THE STORY OF THE EKIPA

Decorative buttons carved from ivory were worn by Ovambo women to demonstrate their status and show off their husbands' wealth. Some men had many wives and adorned them all with *ekipas*. First noted around the end of the nineteenth century, when they were seen on the wives and daughters of chiefs and headmen in southern Angola, *ekipas* were important as status symbols, though sometimes used to pay for food and necessities purchased from the Ovambos in northern Namibia.

To make *ekipas*, elephant tusks purchased from hunters were cut into small pieces and buried for several weeks in ground dampened with animal urine to achieve the desired golden brown color. After the proper color was obtained, the Ovambos carved the ivory into slightly domed oval, round, square, multi-cornered, or oblong shapes, about 2 inches 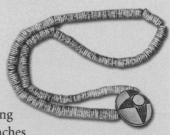 across and ¾ inch thick. Each *ekipa* was then decorated with a carved, usually geometric, border. Finally, the *ekipas* were polished with sandstone and rubbed with a kind of aloe gel before being treated with *okalula,* a red ochre substance that highlighted the carved areas with a darker color. Ivory *ekipas* were preferred, but some were made from hippo tooth or bone, and occasionally from wood or the makalani palm nut, which is known as "vegetable ivory."

The *ekipas* were often attached to strips of elephant hide by two holes on the back, like those of a button. The hide strips were worn as belts, often featuring as many as a dozen *ekipas*; sometimes two or more strips hung down vertically from a belt and, if the woman's husband was rich, those strips held more *ekipas.* They were always worn on special occasions, such as *enfundula* (young girls' initiation ceremonies) and weddings.

With the arrival of the Christian missionaries, displaying too much skin was frowned upon, thus changing both the Ovambo women's style of dress and decorative ornamentation. Today, collectors treasure antique *ekipas* and they are often seen combined with gold or silver and tourmalines in contemporary jewelry in Namibian shops.

hats decorated with beads are made by women at the Queen Sofia Resettlement Farm. Pambili products are also sold at the Omba Gallery in the Namibia Craft Center.

Souvenirs

These can be found in gift shops all over Namibia, as well as in shops maintained in the Namibian Wildlife Resorts properties. Some shops sell higher-end items, such as hand-stitched linens, along with a variety of gift items. Most lodges have their own gift shops.

MUSEUMS, GALLERIES, AND CULTURAL SITES

Namibians of all backgrounds are committed to the preservation of their history and culture and support a variety of museums around the country. Schoolchildren are taken to see displays commemorating various events in the country's history, and visitors to Namibia will find the museums of interest.

The **National Museum of Namibia** in Windhoek houses more than two million items of cultural and historical significance in two display facilities, the Alte Feste Museum and the Owela Museum.

The **TransNamib Museum** is located in the historical Windhoek Railway Station and contains artifacts of cultural interest, including an Illing locomotive, one of the first used in the country.

The **Geological Survey Museum** in Windhoek houses minerals, fossils, and meteorites, mining maps, ore samples, and photographs.

The **Swakopmund Museum** in the old Customs House displays collections important to coastal development in Namibia, as well as information about the natural history of the Namib Desert and cultural anthropology of Namibia's ethnic groups.

The **Walvis Bay Museum** offers displays about the early domestic and commercial developments in this port city.

The **Lüderitz Museum** is of particular interest to those interested in the early Portuguese expeditions, the mining of diamonds, and the history of the area. The outdoor courtyard contains colonial-era wagons, whalebones, and mining equipment.

East of Lüderitz is the deserted diamond mining town of **Kolmanskop**, where houses still stand from the heady early days after the discovery of the stones.

Other museums that focus upon Namibia's history and early settlement by missionaries and the colonial period include Rehoboth Museum, Duwisib Castle, and the Keetmanshoop Museum in a restored Rheinische Mission, which contains both items reflecting the history of Keetmanshoop and the traditional culture of the Nama people.

Museums, displays, and cultural sites devoted to traditional culture include:

Uukwaluudhi Traditional Homestead at Tsandi, where the Ovambo king of the area still lives;

Nakambale Museum in Ovamboland at Olukonda, exhibitions on the site of the first Nakambale church, which was built in 1870 by the first Finnish missionaries;

Historic Living Museum at Grashoek in Bushmanland offers visitors the opportunity to meet traditionally dressed Ju/Hoansi San people;

Naukluft Foundation in the Nama community of Nabasib, where Nama culture can be seen.

Galleries are located in major towns and cities and show/sell paintings, photography, prints, and handicrafts of particular artistic or cultural importance. In 2007, during the celebration of the centenary of Etosha National Park, a number of outdoor installations produced by emerging Namibian artists were shown, setting the stage for future public exhibitions.

MUSIC AND THE PERFORMING ARTS

Music is central to the expression of culture in African societies and Namibia is no exception. Traditional tribal music uses instruments created from gourds, bowls, and hair from the tails of cattle or plant fibers. The Nama are especially known for their creative handcrafted instruments, which are technically advanced. In the north of

Namibia, Ovambo and Kavango use drums widely, even at religious services. In Caprivi, xylophones were created using gourds and reeds. The Bushmen use dance as an expression of spirituality and to promote healing and a sense of community. The traditional dances and songs are passed down from generation to generation. Church music was an integral part of the Christian missionary movement and plays a big role in the independent African churches, where four-part harmony is sung *a cappella* (without instruments).

The German colonists brought with them a love for classical music. They were joined in the organization of musical societies, choral groups, and concerts by the English and Afrikaners who migrated to Namibia. Visiting opera companies and symphony orchestras from around the world draw crowds of music lovers to Windhoek's national theater complex. The State Music Conservatory was founded in Windhoek in 1971 and the first mixed race chorus was formed in the 1980s.

SPORTS

Soccer is the game played by young people in dusty clearings and grassy fields all over Namibia, sometimes with a ball made of twine. The country's soccer, rugby, and cricket teams play internationally, as well as to big local crowds. Track and field have become popular since Namibian Frankie Fredericks won medals at the Barcelona Olympics in 1992.

Riding is an important individual sport and Namibians often win at international competitions; horseback safaris are popular with good riders. There are tennis courts in most towns and golf courses in Windhoek and Swakopmund. Freshwater and saltwater angling is excellent and waterskiing is popular on various man-made lakes.

Namibia is ideal for adventure sports, which include kite- and windsurfing, ATVing, sand boarding on the dunes, paragliding and microlighting, trekking, camel safaris, motorcycle safaris, rappeling, mountain biking, canoeing, rafting, diving, ballooning, gliding, and skydiving.

WILDLIFE
Endangered and Unique Animal Species
Namibia is home to several endangered species, and because there is such a diversity of habitats, there are several unique species of animal specially adapted to the desert. It is one of the few countries where six species of large carnivore live. As we have seen, nature and the protection of the environment are core values to Namibians, who

take great pride in their wildlife and natural resources. Those groups who have historically been in conflict with animals are finding an effective balance between man and nature as they seek the benefits that come with responsible conservation and tourism.

The Desert Elephants are a group of elephants in northwest Namibia that have adapted to the sparse food and water of a desert environment. These elephants, while anatomically the same as other African elephants, have learned to climb high mountains and to travel for three days without water in order to reach a new food source. It is amazing to track these elephants and find them balanced halfway up a rocky mountain where they have found a plant they like to eat. African elephants that live in areas traditional to the species may be seen at Etosha National Park, as well as in the Caprivi Strip. They can create havoc on small farms in northern Namibia when foraging for food at night.

The black rhino is an endangered species, the largest unfenced population of which is in northwest Namibia. Through the efforts of the Namibian government, local communities, and NGOs such as the Rhino Trust, the numbers have increased to about 400 from a low of fifty. These animals have adapted to the arid environment and can go four days without water; most other black rhinos will rarely stray more than six to eight miles from a water source. The favorite food of this species is the extremely poisonous euphorbia plant. (Namibia also has a population of white rhinos. To tell the difference, look at the mouth. The black rhino has a pointed upper lip, while the white rhino has a wide, square mouth. The difference between them is not actually color.)

Namibia has the largest population of cheetahs, an endangered species, in the world and two organizations, the AfriCat Foundation and the Cheetah Conservation Fund, focus on research, education, and animal welfare. Both NGOs are located near Otjiwarongo; AfriCat has lodging facilities and CCF offers day tours.

The brown hyena, an extremely rare carnivore, lives in the Namib and Kalahari Deserts. Along the Skeleton Coast of Namibia, it feeds mainly on seals. It does not need water, as it receives

moisture from its prey, and has adapted well to the desert environment. Namibia has the only population of Hartmann's mountain zebra, a subspecies of the mountain zebra. They can be seen in the Namib Naukluft Park, in Damaraland, the Skeleton Coast Park, and Kaokoland (the Kunene).

The oryx (*gemsbok*) is one of the antelopes best adapted to desert life and can be seen throughout Namibia. When the oryx's body temperature rises in extreme heat, its brain has a mechanism to cool it down. The oryx gets water from its diet, but will come to water holes to drink.

Other Mammals

Other mammals found in Namibia include the springbok, suricate (meerkat), the bat-eared fox, aardvark (anteater, or ant bear), giraffe, gnu (blue wildebeest), Damara dik-dik, buffalo, warthog, leopard, lion, wild dog, caracal, honey badger, impala, baboon, kudu,  and many more. The wild horses of Namibia, possible descendants of horses abandoned by German colonial soldiers, can be seen in the south near Klein Aus.

Marine Life

Namibia's marine mammals are protected after culling wiped out large numbers of whales, dolphins, and seals in the nineteenth century. The largest colonies of Cape fur seals in Africa are found here, 67 percent of the world's Cape fur seal population. (They are actually classified as sea lions.) Namibia harvests approximately 2 percent of the Cape fur seal population annually as a conservation effort; pelts, oil, and meat are all utilized. The Heaviside's dolphin, also known as the Benguela dolphin because it rides the Benguela Current, is commonly seen in the Walvis Bay lagoon.

Birds
Namibia is a bird-watcher's paradise—almost 650 species of birds are found here due to the diverse range of habitats. The endemic, or near endemic, species include Hartlaug's francolin, Ruppell's korhaan, Damara tern, Ruppell's parrot, violet woodhoopoe, Monteiro's hornbill, dune lark, Barlow's lark, Gray's lark, black tit, bare-cheeked babbler, Herero chat, rockrunner, and whitetailed shrike. The best time for bird-watching is in the summer months (November to April). The greatest diversity of birds can be seen at Etosha National Park, the Caprivi Strip, and Waterberg Plateau Park.

Other birds that can be seen in great numbers in Namibia include the ostrich, which roams wild in most of Namibia, and the sociable weaver, which makes huge communal nests. There is a waterbird sanctuary near Walvis Bay.

Reptiles

There are almost 70 endemic species among the 258 recognized reptile species living in Namibia, including 55 lizards and geckos, ten snakes, and one tortoise. Among the most interesting are the shovel-nosed lizard, which collects its water from the coastal fog that permeates the desert; the Namaqua chameleon, which forages on the beaches and spits out excess salt; and the Peringuey's adder ("sidewinder"), a rare snake that lives in the dunes of the Namib Desert and undulates sideways over the hot sand.

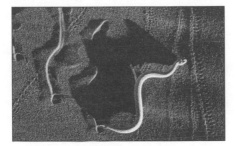

Of the ninety species of snake found in the country, seventeen are poisonous. Snakes are important to the Namibian ecosystem and may be killed only when they create a danger. Among the poisonous snakes in Namibia are the puff adder, the Namib dune adder, the horned adder, the mole adder, the Cape cobra, the Western black-spitting cobra, the zebra snake, the black-necked spitting cobra, the Angolan cobra, and the black mamba. A useful tip: wildlife experts say that no striped Namibian snakes are dangerous.

Insects
About 50,000 species of insect have been cataloged in Namibia, 1,541 of them endemic to the country, but experts believe that number represents no more than 20 percent of what is out there. Unusual insects include the "tok-tokkie" (desert tenebrionid beetle), which has adapted to life in the desert dunes by means of "fog-basking," collecting moisture by standing on its head and letting condensed water from the fog run down its body into its mouth. The wheeling spider, which lives in the dunes, escapes from predators by tucking its legs underneath, curling into a ball and rolling down the slope of the dune at 1.5 meters per second. When rolling away is not an option, it copies the movement of the dancing white lady spider, and "dances" across the dunes. Another interesting spider in Namibia is the Roman or sun spider, which can be huge (four inches or more across), red and hairy, but which is actually harmless. Afrikaners say the spider seems to chase after humans, but is really running after the

moving shadow. The Namas call this spider the "barber" spider because of its huge fangs. They say if you sleep on the ground, this spider will come and cut your hair. Other insects in Namibia include a variety of scorpions and the "creepy crawly," a giant centipede with red body and orange legs, which has poisonous fangs. The Shongololo, the giant African millipede, is harmless, which is a good thing, because it can grow up to twelve inches long.

Plants
Considering the arid environment, it is amazing that Namibia has almost 700 endemic species of plants, including dozens of colorful desert-growing lichens. The most interesting is undoubtedly the *Welwitschia*, which lives in the Namib Desert and is one of the oldest plants on earth. Some plants live to be more than 2,000 years old, producing only two leaves, which split and curl in the wind. The quiver tree, a type of aloe with a distinctive silhouette, grows in southern Namibia and is sometimes the only tree for miles.

TEN SITES NOT TO MISS IN NAMIBIA

- The rock paintings at Twyfelfontein, named a UNESCO World Heritage Site in 2007
- Sossusvlei, the incredible dune ocean within the Namib-Naukluft Park, where dunes may reach heights of 330 feet (100 m).
- Etosha National Park, one of Africa's largest game reserves (8,600 sq. miles /22,270 sq. km).
- Cape Cross Seal Reserve and the Skeleton Coast Park—300,000 Cape fur seals jostle for space on the rock and dive for fish in the Atlantic; remote and intriguing, the Skeleton Coast Park ranges 250 miles north from Cape Cross along the windswept Atlantic coast.
- Fish River Canyon and Ai-Ais Resort—the second-largest natural gorge in the world, this deep and rugged canyon is 100 miles (160 km) long and up to 1,600 feet (550 m) deep and is a favorite route for adventure trekking.

- The Caprivi Strip—hippos, water buffalo, elephants, crocodiles, African fish eagles, and more than 400 species of bird can be seen in the various parks of the Caprivi: the Mudumu, Mangetti Game Camp, Mamili National Park, Mahango Game Park, Caprivi Game Park, and the adjacent Khaudum Game Park, which is only for 4x4 access.

- Sandwich Harbor and Walvis Bay lagoon— these lagoons comprise the most important wetland area on the southern African coast.

- Waterberg Plateau Park—the imposing red sandstone formation, the Waterberg Plateau, is home to twenty-five game and more than two hundred bird species.

- Swakopmund—this strange little German town on the Atlantic Coast was the site of the arrival of early colonists, who then traveled for months in covered wagons to reach the capital, Windhoek, or the mines of northern Namibia. It is an oasis and vacation playground, offering salt air, cool breezes, distinctive architecture, and fresh seafood.

- Windhoek—Namibia's capital is more than a jumping-off point for a safari; it is an interesting and vibrant city, where a cross-section of Namibians live, work, and play. There is excellent shopping and a variety of high quality restaurants. Here, one may visit Katutura, where many black Namibians have created a buzzing community, or see the historic German buildings, including three Bavarian castles, that were built in the late nineteenth century.

chapter seven

TRAVEL, HEALTH, & SAFETY

BORDER CROSSINGS AND ENTRY REQUIREMENTS

Foreign nationals must enter Namibia on a passport that is valid for at least six months after the date of entry. Visas are required for all visitors, except nationals of countries with which Namibia has agreements. Tourists may remain in the country for ninety days; business visas are also granted for ninety days.

There are thirty border crossings between Namibia and its four neighbors: Botswana, Angola, Zambia, and South Africa. Documentary proof of ownership and a police clearance are required for private vehicles, while a letter of authorization from the owner (or rental agency in the case of rental cars) is necessary if the vehicle is not registered in the driver's name. Cross-border charges apply for most vehicles and sometimes the purchase of additional insurance will be necessary before entering another country.

Air service into Namibia from abroad includes regular flights between points in Germany and Gatwick, London. Direct air links to major sub-

Saharan points, such as Cape Town and Johannesburg, Luanda, Lusaka, and Harare connect with international flights from Europe, the USA, Australia, and other places. Air Namibia, the national airline, operates two Airbus planes between London, Frankfurt, and Windhoek.

GETTING AROUND

Only 23 percent of Namibians have a car; those without depend upon formal or informal public transportation to get around. More and more Namibians in rural areas are using bicycles, especially schoolchildren who receive them from the Michelle McLean Children's Trust, formed by Miss Universe 1992 to provide assistance to needy children in her home country. In remote areas, mules or horses are used to pull wagons, some of which are constructed using the beds of old pickup trucks.

Intra-Namibian public transportation can be crowded, as many people work in Windhoek, for example, and travel home weekends and holidays to the far north. Generally, they don't bring along animals on these journeys. There is often laughter and conversation along the long trip, with stops to pick up hitchhikers in remote areas.

Air Service

Air Namibia offers domestic flights into eleven airports with immigration and customs facilities.

General Aviation (private aircraft) makes up much of the traffic within Namibia, especially for those wishing to do fly-in safaris to remote areas or who have limited time. Pilots are well trained and planes well maintained. Namibia has 200 registered airstrips.

Road Travel

Self-drive, independent safaris are very popular among tourists, as they are an excellent way to see the country. Driving is on the left-hand side and

drivers are expected to carry their original driver's licenses. Using cell phones while driving is illegal. There are about 26,000 miles (42,000 km) of maintained roads, of which about 15 percent are surfaced with bitumen. The Association for Safe International Road Travel rates Namibian roads as among the best in sub-Saharan Africa, and road signs are international and well placed. Roads along the coast are often "salt" roads. Careful driving rules must be obeyed when driving on gravel roads; most rental car companies provide explicit instructions for how to drive on them and charge above-average insurance excesses.

Four-wheel drive is unnecessary except in certain remote areas or during heavy rainy seasons. Both diesel and unleaded fuel are readily available.

Special attention should be paid to signs warning of animals crossing, especially when driving at dusk. If an animal, such as a kudu antelope, appears in the road, stop the car and turn off headlights. Otherwise, the animal may be blinded by the lights and run into the car, which can cause damage or death both to the animal and to the occupants of the car. When the animal has moved on, you may continue.

Turning right on a red traffic light is not permitted in Namibia. Seat belts are required for all vehicle occupants, but often pickup trucks ("*bakkies*") will be seen with the occupants of the cab buckled up and the back full of people without seats, much less seat belts.

Motorcyclists are required by law to wear protective helmets. While child car seats are not required, they are recommended.

To drive legally while in Namibia, visitors staying more than a month should have an international driving permit, though it is a good idea to obtain one whenever driving in a foreign country for any period of time is part of an itinerary. Legally, short-term visitors do not need an international driving permit; a valid driver's license is sufficient.

Most major roads are two-way and undivided (no center divider or median), with one lane going in each direction. Drivers should remain alert for passing vehicles and exercise caution when passing slow-moving vehicles. Often there are dips in the road, which may obscure oncoming traffic—be careful when passing another car in these circumstances.

Accidents involving drunk drivers are an increasing problem on major roads, where there are higher speed limits. Driving under the influence is illegal in Namibia. A charge of manslaughter can be made against a driver involved in an accident resulting in death.

Travelers have learned over the years that when a problem with the car occurs, the next Namibian to arrive on the scene will always stop to help. The safest option when stranded with car trouble is to wait inside the car, out of the heat and away from possible predators.

Seeing the Sights Alone
Namibia is a very safe country overall, but driving it alone can involve long stretches of empty road. If an accident or emergency were to occur, it would be safer to have at least one companion. Cell phone service is improving, but still does not cover the entire country. Solo travelers are welcomed at lodges and resorts, however, whether they arrive alone or with a tour group. Those who are traveling alone can hire a private plane and pilot to go from place to place, or engage a car and driver. Otherwise, if a large tour bus is not of interest, there are small, more personalized tours available with guides and few people in the group.

Hitchhiking
Hitchhiking is common in Namibia, especially in remote areas, where many people don't have cars. If traveling in a rural area, where mothers and children or elderly couples stand along the road waiting for a ride, many people will stop and offer

HELP ON THE ROAD

Namibians are among the most helpful people on Earth when it comes to assisting people with car trouble on isolated roads. One hot afternoon, as we were driving in a sedan car to a lodge near Omaruru, we came upon a wide, dry riverbed. Halfway across, we got stuck in the sand. We tried letting some air out of the tires to obtain more traction, to no avail. Next, we looked in vain for pieces of wood large enough to wedge under the tires, in hopes that might help. Finally, we decided to wait for someone to come along.

About twenty minutes later, a car came from the opposite direction. Inside were two young men, a woman, and a child and they immediately asked how they could help. It was quickly agreed that one of the men would stay with my husband and the car, while I would go with the others the twenty kilometers to the lodge to ask for a truck to come and pull us out.

An hour later, we arrived back at the riverbed, followed by the truck. There seemed to be a party going on—three other cars had stopped to help and our car was now out of the sand and ready to go. The crowd— black, white, Namibian, European, South African— chatted and laughed together while they waited for our return. Once they saw all was well, everyone got back in their cars, waved good-bye, and continued on their journeys.

them a ride to the next town. The country is so large that Namibians are accustomed to helping each other out in this way. Visitors who choose to pick up hitchhikers often learn more about the people and the country during the trip—though this activity is by personal choice only.

Those wanting rides must consider the possibility of intoxicated and/or reckless drivers, along with the poor mechanical condition of some motor vehicles. Hitchhiking should be carefully considered before trying it.

TOURS

A variety of tours are offered in Namibia: scheduled tours in luxury coaches, private tours in microbuses, fly-in safaris, specialized tailor-made tours (bird-watching, fishing, hunting, geology, etc.), horseback, camel, or motorcycle safaris, white-water rafting, 4x4 safaris into remote areas, and train tours. Day tours are available in most major cities and towns and include cultural township tours as a way to experience Namibia's many ethnic groups.

Rail

There are several rail trips available to tourists or other travelers, such as the Desert Express, which offers an overnight scenic journey between Windhoek and Swakopmund. There is scheduled passenger service between Windhoek and Walvis

Bay, and Windhoek and Oshivelo in northern
Namibia. There are 1,550 miles (2,500 km) of
narrow-gauge track making up several branches
of railway.

Bus
Several companies operate a private bus service
from Windhoek to Cape Town, Johannesburg,
Victoria Falls, Botswana, Zambia, and points
around the country; there is no public bus service.

Taxis
Taxis are operated twenty-four hours a day in
Windhoek and private operators offer registered
taxi service between Hosea Kutako International
Airport and Windhoek. Radio taxis that display
the NABTA logo (Namibia Bus and Taxi
Association) are the most reliable.

Cruises
Cruise lines sail in and out of Walvis Bay and
sometimes stop at Lüderitz. There are several
choices of day cruises in the Walvis Bay Lagoon,
where visitors look for whales, seals, and dolphins.

WHERE TO STAY
Namibia has a variety of accommodation for
tourists, ranging from rough camping on the
ground to four-star luxury. Properties registered
with the Namibian Tourism Board are graded on a

system similar to those in South Africa and Europe. The types of establishments include campsites, hotels, hotel pensions, guest farms, lodges, guest houses, permanent tented camps and tented lodges, and rest camps. The Namibian Wildlife Resorts division of the Ministry of Environment and Tourism operates lodges and camps in or near national parks and preserves. In addition, there are backpackers' hostels, bed and breakfasts, and self-catering accommodation. The Namibian Tourism Board Web site at www.namibiatourism.com.na provides information on accommodation throughout the country.

NATIONAL PARKS AND PRIVATE PRESERVES

The Ministry of Environment and Tourism (MET) manages almost twenty national reserves and game parks, among them Etosha National Park, Fish River Canyon, Skeleton Coast Park, and

Namib-Naukluft Park. In addition, there are 182 privately owned nature preserves, including NamibRand Game Reserve (at 445,000 acres, or 180,000 hectares, it is the largest private conservation area in Africa), Gondwana Canon Park (252,000 acres, or 102,000 hectares), and Huab Private Nature Reserve (19,900 acres, or 8,060 hectares). Government-authorized concession areas, such as Klein Aus Vista, a separate part of Gondwana, operate tourism activities under strict guidelines.

HEALTH
Travelers should be aware that medical care is excellent in the towns, but harder to come by in remote areas. The towns have state-run hospitals; well-equipped clinics service smaller towns and villages. Private hospitals are located in Windhoek (three, with intensive care, MRI, kidney dialysis, ICU), Tsumeb, Otjiwarongo, Walvis Bay, and Swakopmund. All specialist fields are available in Windhoek, where 90 percent of emergency cases can be treated.

All medication is available in Windhoek; US Food and Drug Administration standards are strictly adhered to and the local Drug Control Board controls all imported medicines. People planning travel to the north should consider taking antimalaria medicines and carry insect repellents and sprays. Most of Namibia is not a malaria area.

Emergency evacuation services are provided by International SOS Namibia, which is equipped to reach remote areas very quickly. If traveling cross-country by car, always take along a first aid kit, including a "space" blanket to provide insulation from heat or cold and to use as a reflector to attract emergency flights or planes passing overhead.

As we have noted, HIV/AIDS is a serious problem in Namibia. Safe sex precautions should be taken at all times.

SAFETY

Namibia has a well-trained police force and is a relatively safe and crime-free destination. The most common crimes are opportunistic thefts, including pickpocketing, purse snatching, vehicle theft, and vehicle break-ins. Violent crimes are much less frequent than nonviolent incidents. Commonsense measures such as being alert to one's surroundings, avoiding isolated areas of town, not leaving valuables in parked cars, keeping car doors locked and windows up while driving, and safeguarding purses, wallets, and especially cellular phones are the best deterrents against becoming a victim. Walking in groups after dark in towns is generally safe, but avoid unlit areas.

chapter eight

BUSINESS BRIEFING

The Namibian government's policy of national reconciliation after Independence in 1990 was essential to the preservation of the existing business structure, which was primarily run by whites, as well as to the development of business and of black economic empowerment in the future. In the almost two decades since Independence, business in Namibia has continued to grow and some segments of the population that had never before had access to business opportunities have entered the workforce.

GOVERNMENT POLICY

The Ministry of Trade and Industry, through its four divisions, pursues objectives that recognize the critical role of the private sector as an engine of economic growth. Development of the economy is fostered by the creation of a business-friendly environment and the stimulation of the private sector via legislative instruments; the provision of industrial infrastructure, such as the Trans-Kalahari and Trans-Caprivi highways;

export and investment promotion; and the provision of affordable credit facilities.

The Namibian Investment Centre (NIC) is charged with attracting foreign investment and provides services to potential and current investors, including interaction with various ministries to minimize bureaucratic obstacles. Commercial counselors representing the NIC work overseas at various Namibian embassies and offices.

The NIC works closely with the Offshore Development Company, managers of the tax-free export processing zone. Namibian-based entrepreneurs are offered tax incentives for investment in the manufacturing and reexport sectors, in particular for export into the Southern African Customs Union.

The third directorate is responsible for domestic trade, while the fourth, the Directorate of International Trade, works with trade policy, multilateral trade organizations, and import/export management.

The Small Business Credit Guarantee Trust supports the development and growth of small enterprises, and assists small entrepreneurs in obtaining financing for their projects, at times guaranteeing up to 80 percent of principal loan amounts. The Development Bank of Namibia assists

private and public sector enterprises in their start-up phases. Major cities and various regions also offer business start-up support.

THE BUSINESS COMMUNITY

Private business is the backbone of the Namibian economy, while government is the biggest employer. The country is considered one of the least bureaucratic places to do business in Africa. While most business owners were white at Independence in 1990, today more and more small, medium, and large businesses are owned by blacks. There is also an increase in businesses owned by foreigners, especially those coming from Asia.

After agriculture, the retail sector employs most Namibians. Retail in Namibia ranges from chains and big box stores owned by South African interests, to large local retailers, thousands of small market stalls, and stores run by individuals. Today, more and more of these vendors are Chinese, who have come to Africa to take advantage of both the large investments made by Chinese industry and the opportunity to sell low-priced goods in Namibia.

Small entrepreneurs are a growth sector of Namibian business, providing income for families in remote areas who benefit from tourism and assistance from NGOs. Handmade crafts (baskets, wood carvings, jewelry, embroidered linens, Karakul rugs, dolls, and other items) are sold along remote roads, as well as in open-air markets and craft cooperatives in villages, towns, and cities. Several NGOs and private companies have brought these goods to market in large metropolitan areas, such as Windhoek, and have exported them to countries such as Germany.

The Namibian version of the convenience store is often called the "Portuguese store," because many are owned by Portuguese who immigrated to Namibia after Angolan independence from Portugal. The *cuca* bar is a combination bar and market found primarily in the north and run by local entrepreneurs, who often give their bars colorful names. Overall, Namibia's retailers offer much more than some other countries in the region, except for South Africa, including imported as well as locally produced items.

Namibia has long had significant representation from the South African banking, insurance, and manufacturing sector. In addition, there are banks and financial service companies that date back a century, to the time of German rule. Today, many financial service companies are owned and/or managed locally, but some retain not only major South African shareholders, but Chinese as well. Several large, locally owned holding companies have built business interests in multiple sectors, such as food and fishing, beverages, retail, information technology, banking, and communications.

Other sectors with longtime international investment are mining, petroleum, freight and port services, and fishing. After Independence, the Namibian government became a partner in the diamond mining industry, which had previously been controlled entirely by De Beers. Most manufacturing and extraction companies have a high percentage of local managers.

Large local businesses, in particular tanneries of exotic skins, have entered the retail market, as well as continued to sell wholesale. There is an increasing demand from upscale hospitality projects for locally made furniture and decorative items.

PROMOTING RACIAL DIVERSITY

Being a multicultural country, Namibia promotes and expects diversity. Racial diversity in business has become the norm since Independence, due both to affirmative action policies and to laws designed to assist formerly disadvantaged groups in entrepreneurial ventures. A BEE (black economic empowerment) law is still in the draft stages, but local businesses are already adopting it as official company policy.

Though a working democracy, Namibia is known as a "patronage state," where family, friends, and political allies often receive preference for political appointments or jobs. Tribal diversity in the workplace is often a function of both population and politics, depending upon where in the country the job is located. The political party in power since Independence, SWAPO, is made up mainly of Ovambo, the largest tribe in Namibia, whose members populate most of the cities to the north, as well as having a large presence in Windhoek, the capital. Therefore, many Ovambo have been appointed to positions of power in the government, gained through the election of a SWAPO majority (74 percent in 2004), though Damara and Herero are also well represented. In business and the civil service, there is some effort to recruit from a variety of tribes and races, as there is at lower levels in the public sector.

WOMEN IN BUSINESS

Women continue to struggle for equal pay—in 2005, they were paid 50 percent less than men, although women head 39 percent of urban and 44 percent of rural households. They make up

27 percent of managers in the public sector and 27 percent of members of Parliament. Laws and policies in place under South African rule, which forbade married women from opening bank accounts without having their husbands' permission or from making loans for their own businesses, have been changed. In addition, women are gaining a foothold as managers in businesses, as well as excelling at small entrepreneurial projects. Women have played a major role in government since Independence, including serving as Ministers in the cabinet, as well as in other areas of the public sector.

CORRUPTION

Transparency International ranked Namibia forty-ninth out of 159 countries in 2005 for corruption. Namibia received a score of 4.7 out of 10 (with a score of 10 meaning "highly clean"), which indicates that corruption is a problem. The Public Integrity Index rated the country "weak." That said, some research shows that the *perception* of corruption in Namibia is actually worse than the reality. In fact, the country ranks higher than other Africa countries in systems put in place to control corruption; government institutions include the Anti Corruption Commission, the Office of the Ombudsman, and the Office of the Auditor General. Sam Nujoma, the first president of Namibia, declared a zero tolerance campaign against corruption, but, as former chief of state, is himself embroiled in investigations into payoffs, as are several members of government ministries. Yet, corruption in Namibia is not as prevalent as in other countries in the region. Two areas where it has been a problem are the extractive sector (mining), where it is widely thought that payoffs have occurred, and the diamond industry, where some small companies set up to buy and sell diamonds are thought to be money laundering.

Corruption is held in check by a strong media, the most important scrutinizing institution in Namibia. And it should be noted that what may sometimes appear to be corruption to Westerners can have quite a different connotation in a culture where tribal leaders have the traditional duty to promote the well-being of family and clan members.

TEAM NAMIBIA

Launched in 2004, Team Namibia is an organization of Namibian companies and companies who have invested in Namibia who promote the "Be Namibian—Buy Namibian" campaign. Members encourage corporate social responsibility and compliance with legislative and environmental standards, and are allowed to carry the product/service logo of Team Namibia. The ultimate goal is to protect and create jobs for local production.

MAKING CONTACT

Doing your homework before arriving in Namibia is key to the success of a business trip. The country is huge and distances are long, so before potentially wasting time and effort on cold calls, spend some time pinpointing areas of interest and make contact in advance.

The success of cold-calling in Namibia is iffy—when the person you wish to see is available, he or she will invariably be friendly and welcoming. However, follow-up may be lacking since there has been no time for them to establish your credentials or to prepare for your visit. Cold calls on government officials should be avoided—at the very least, ask for help from your embassy's trade representative in Windhoek before trying to see a government minister or functionary without an appointment. Do this kind of thing only if you are in Namibia for another reason and plan to come back for serious business discussion.

THE IMPORTANCE OF PERSONAL RELATIONSHIPS

Many Afrikaner and German Namibians whose families have been in the country for generations or who have gone to school together have close ties within the business community. The same can be said of tribal connections, especially as blacks are seeking to give—and get—a leg up in a society that was for many years racially divided. The bottom line is the bottom line—if an outsider has something to offer that is interesting from a business point of view, and does not directly compete with their own enterprises, businesspeople want to listen.

How do you win trust? A step at a time, by maintaining open and aboveboard business practices, delivering what you say you will, and negotiating contracts that are fair to both sides.

The bible of trade and industry in Namibia is the Namibia Trade Directory, which can be obtained through Namibian embassies or consulates around the world or via the Web site, www.namibiatradedirectory.com, where various portions may be downloaded or the entire directory ordered. The directory is 250 pages of company profiles, including management names and photos; government contacts, statistics, and information about every sector of the economy.

Namibian embassies, consular services, and honorary consuls of Namibia in your own country can be quite helpful in setting up business appointments and making introductions for business-related activities in Namibia. Embassies and consulates of your own country located in Namibia should be visited as soon as you arrive (make such appointments in advance); this is where you may get some unvarnished information about potential for success, the best people to see, and where any of your compatriots may have succeeded or failed.

The Namibia Chamber of Commerce and Industry (http://www.ncci.org.na/home.aspx) has offices around the country. Taking a look at their Web site before arriving can be helpful in planning whom to see and where to go. The NCCI assists its members in attending trade shows and international events and can be a good source of information about when Namibian businesspeople may be in your country. It can be a good idea to make personal contact at a trade show in advance of your trip to Namibia.

DRESS CODE

Unless you are going into a rural area or small town, you should dress for business, at least for the first appointment. Namibians are often very smart dressers and appreciate professional attire. If your host wears no tie or jacket, you can do likewise for the next meeting. Women don't usually wear tights or stockings, at least in summer, but they do cover their upper arms and dress more conservatively than in other countries. Miniskirts and sleeveless or low-cut blouses are inappropriate for business. Government appointments require business dress.

If you are going into a remote area, such as the headquarters of a mine or to a meeting at a game reserve or lodge, the dress code is more informal—

khaki pants or slacks for both men and women, collared shirt with no tie, and comfortable shoes (not sports shoes) are okay. Take along a jacket or vest, especially if you are going to the coast or expect to be there after dark, when it is much cooler. Appointments in the bush, at a tourist resort, or game reserve do not require a jacket, but long sleeves are important to protect from sun and insects. Wear subdued colors, such as khaki or sage green, in case you are invited for a game drive or a sundowner in the bush.

If you are invited to a formal event, a dark suit with tie or cocktail dress is appropriate. Black-tie events are rare and not every man will wear a tuxedo, though the more sophisticated will do so. Women often wear long dresses to black-tie events. Traditional dress is also acceptable and welcomed at these events, adding color and interest to the occasion.

GREETINGS

The business atmosphere in Namibia is similar to Western Europe, a bit more formal at the beginning, with a more relaxed interaction later. Handshakes are the norm and can range from Western European or American style to traditional African style, particularly after you get to know a colleague. Usual Western European business etiquette applies. Be sure to shake hands with everyone again before leaving. Business is generally conducted in English, although Afrikaans and German may also be spoken.

Business cards should be exchanged at the outset of a meeting. Information on the card should include both electronic and physical contact information, as well as titles. They should be prepared in English. Keep to traditional business style.

If you are going to see a tribal chief in a remote area, you should take someone with you who knows the protocol. In some settings, you should wait for your host to speak first, for example. Let your host take the lead and don't be surprised by a very long handshake and greeting.

If the person you are meeting is a government minister, call him Mr. or Ms. Minister. If he or she is an ambassador, call him or her Your Excellency. Do not call anyone by their first name until and unless you are asked to—in a multicultural society, some people are more formal than others and it is better to err on the side of formality.

ENTERTAINING BUSINESS COLLEAGUES

Eating, drinking, and socializing are an important part of building business relationships. If you are working in Windhoek, Walvis Bay, or Swakopmund, you will find a variety of excellent restaurants in which to entertain colleagues over lunch or dinner, many with private dining rooms.

Lunches are generally shorter, as people don't stay away from their offices more than an hour or so unless there is a conference or other event.

You may be asked to visit a business colleague's farm or beach house for a weekend. If you accept, you should bring a house gift, such as a nonpersonal item from your home country or a bottle of good wine. If you are invited to dinner, you should bring a gift for the hostess.

PUNCTUALITY

Being on time is important. Business hours are usually 9:00 a.m. to 5:00 p.m. Monday to Friday. It is best when scheduling meetings with government officials to make appointments on Wednesdays and Thursdays when possible, to avoid conflicting with staff meetings or early departures for the weekend.

Depending upon whom you are meeting, your appointment may or may not start on time; nevertheless, *you* should be there on time. Bring along something to read or work on and settle in comfortably if you are going to a meeting in a government office, as those appointments are known for starting late. On the other hand, businesses are run on a time-is-money-basis and most appointments will begin when scheduled.

Although Namibians have a strong work ethic, attuned to the cycles of nature as in other agrarian societies, this does not always translate into a sense of urgency at the office.

MEETINGS

Come to business meetings prepared and ready to discuss details, as well as general concepts. Follow the lead of the host, who may engage in general chitchat before getting down to business. Be ready to answer questions.

Presentations

Provide everyone at the meeting with hard copies of your presentation, written in simple English rather than esoteric terminology that may not be understood. Use graphics to illustrate major points. Ask beforehand if PowerPoint or similar presentation systems are encouraged or welcomed—some offices may not be equipped to handle them. Speak in well-articulated English. Be open to questions.

Negotiations

As a rule, Namibians are not aggressive and do not welcome hard-sell tactics. Make clear what you want from your host and how you plan to deliver, produce, or pay for it, without pushing too hard. Set a time for the next meeting or the next step before leaving and follow up to be certain there is no confusion. You may have to make several trips or stay longer to accomplish your goals.

Namibian businesses are generally hierarchical, with final decisions made at the top. In most cases, all sides and opinions will be heard. When you are negotiating a contract, you should be prepared to wait for an answer unless you are meeting with the owner of the company. Silence should not be considered acquiescence. Some people in government may put off making decisions until they are certain there is no downside. Patience is required in these situations.

CONTRACTS AND DISPUTES

You will want to have a written contract, and it is important to hire a local attorney when drawing one up. Namibia's legal system is characterized by pluralism. It is a combination of Westminster-style constitutional law, Roman-Dutch common law, customary law, and international law.

Enforcing contracts and settling disputes takes less time in Namibia than in many other African countries. Namibia is ranked 43 out of 178 countries rated by the World Bank on the ease of doing business. It scores higher than Kenya, Tanzania, and Botswana in the area of protecting investors from misuse of corporate funds and related malfeasance.

There is a great deal of respect for the court system in Namibia. In addition, the Professional Arbitration and Mediation Association facilitates labor, commercial, and constructions disputes.

chapter **nine**

COMMUNICATING

LANGUAGE

When English was chosen as the official language in 1990, very few Namibians actually spoke it; by 2005, English was the language most heard in the streets and today most children, as well as their parents, speak it well. There are fourteen languages used by Namibians in total.

Most people in Namibia are bi- and trilingual, with major languages other than English being Afrikaans, German, Oshivambo, Herero, Nama/Damara, and other indigenous languages. With thousands of Chinese now in the country, Asian languages are growing in importance, but have not yet entered the mainstream.

Accents in English are also sometimes difficult to understand because often people have learned the language later in life. In addition, English is now spoken by people whose first languages are entirely different in terms of construction and pronunciation, and which inevitably influence their English construction and pronunciation.

Speak slowly and clearly whenever possible and offer the same patience that Namibians will offer you. The colloquial word for the language is "Namlish," which refers to the distinctly Namibian way of speaking English.

NONCONFRONTATION AND RESPECT

As we have seen, confrontation is not the Namibian way of solving disputes. People are generally easygoing and ask for what they want, sometimes in less than clear terms or very quietly out of politeness. It is important to listen carefully to be certain that what is being said is completely understood by both sides. If not, do not hesitate to ask for an explanation.

We have also seen that speaking first to an older or senior person is considered impolite in many segments of Namibian culture. By the same token, do not use the first name of an older or senior person unless invited to do so.

HUMOR

Humor plays an important part in Namibian culture, although some express it more openly than others. People enjoy making jokes and watching comedy on television. After Independence many American situation comedies featuring black actors, such as Bill Cosby, were aired on Namibian TV. British television productions, such as "Mr. Bean" and "Allo, Allo," have also been popular. Afrikaners, in particular, are known for their ribald sense of humor, which is usually expressed in Afrikaans. Since so many people in Namibia understand Afrikaans, their humorous comments are understood by almost everyone. More importantly, both Afrikaners and black Namibians are able to laugh at themelves and make jokes at their own expense—more so than German or English Namibians.

Translating Namlish

Just after Independence, Queen Elizabeth II visited Namibia, which is a member of the British Commonwealth. Some news anchors at the Namibian Broadcasting Corporation (NBC) were unaccustomed to speaking English and on this occasion it was evident there was some practicing to be done. The news anchor, looking and sounding very serious and professional, announced that "Queen Elizabeth the eleventh and the Duck of Edinburgh" were in town. Today, Namibian news anchors are as polished as any and present the news in both English and Oshivambo.

BODY LANGUAGE

Namibians in general are not aggressive or arrogant, and this is reflected in their body language. They are patient and polite as a rule. Personal space is respected by almost everyone, though tribal life often involves very close living conditions and people stand closer to those they know well. Gestures and facial expressions are generally low key, unless there is a lively discussion taking place or a great joke being told.

THE COMMUNICATIONS REVOLUTION

Like many less developed countries, Namibia jumped straight into the communications age at an advanced level, going from no landlines in some areas to cell phones in a single step. In 2005, there were about 140,000 landlines compared to almost 500,000 cell phones. Cell phone service covers most of the country (about 85 percent) and having a cell phone is an important way for people in remote areas to keep in touch. There are popular pay-as-you-go cell phone cards (ideal for visitors), as well as contracts available. Cell phones have made an enormous impact in a country with vast areas that were previously unreachable by landline.

Those without electricity leave their cell phones at charging stations in local outdoor markets. Much of the population is adept at using SMS (text) messages and, in fact, SMS Letters to the Editor are an important part of the daily Namibian newspaper.

Pay telephones operated by Telecom Namibia are available almost everywhere and offer a reliable service to those without landlines or cell phones.

The Internet is less prevalent, but improving all the time. There were about 80,000 Internet users as of 2007. Broadband and satellite service have become available in the last few years to augment dial-up, with satellite service particularly important to people living on farms and lodges. For those without the means to have their own service, there are Internet cafés widespread in many small towns. The computers may not be state of the art and the

service not speedy, but it is possible to be in touch by e-mail or to surf the net from more far-flung places like Tsumeb, Omaruru, Oshikato, and Otjiwarongo, as well as

the bigger cities. There are several companies offering Internet service in Namibia.

TECHNOLOGY

Despite the fact that a large percentage of the country is still without electricity, technology is well integrated into Namibian business and society. Both local and international companies sell up-to-date computer equipment and services and offer training in how to use technology. Banks offer

Internet banking, and ATMs (cash machines) are located around the country. Medical facilities often share data electronically. More and more classrooms are being outfitted with computers.

THE MEDIA

Namibia is a vibrant country when it comes to newspapers, with several privately owned dailies published in different languages and offering a range of opinions. They include the *Namibian* (English and Oshivambo), *Allgemeine Zeitung* (German), and *Republikein* (Afrikaans). The press is free and not afraid to criticize; it actively puts pressure on the government, industry, and society when issues of importance arise. There is a government-produced newspaper, *New Era*, and a kind of scandal sheet, the *Windhoek Observer*, which makes pithy comments on current events and runs gory photographs of accidents on the front page.

The Namibian Broadcasting Corporation, which is the primary, state-owned channel in Namibia, offers both television and twenty-four-hour radio coverage. In recent years, One Africa Television was created and reaches more than 80 percent of the population with private commercial free-to-air television. Many Namibians also subscribe to MNet, a South African network that provides international news on networks such as CNN and BBC, as well as movies and other programming.

Radio in Namibia is extremely important and is broadcast in a variety of formats and languages around the country. There are dozens of FM stations and most Namibians get their news from the radio.

MAIL

Namibia has a reliable postal service, which is also a bill-paying service for many of its citizens. There are beautifully designed Namibian stamps, which can be purchased as collectibles.

THE IMPACT OF DIPLOMACY

Because Namibia was considered a "child of the United Nations," several dozen embassies were opened upon Independence in 1990. The arrival of a population of foreign diplomats has affected Namibian society by opening up lines of communication that go far beyond the country's borders, creating opportunities for business, education, foreign funding, and multicultural interaction that would have been impossible before.

CONCLUSION

We began our look at Namibian culture in the splendid isolation of this amazing place and went on to meet and understand something of the diverse peoples who live here. Despite the many differences between tribes and ethnic groups, Namibians share a strong work ethic, a sense of humor, a commitment to preserving the environment, and a pride in a country graced with great natural and human resources. Their values and ideals include love of nature, mutual dependence, self-reliance, and a long tradition of fairness. They consider the family as friends and their friends as family, and they share a strong belief in a greater power. Their strong sense of community extends to newcomers, and you will find yourself welcome wherever you go.

Many travelers who visit Namibia discover themselves changed permanently by the experience and want to return. What is it about this strange and wonderful place that draws people back again and again? Surely, it is because we feel at home here so quickly, embraced by both the people and the culture; and seeing these strong people rise to the challenge of living in a harsh, yet beautiful, environment inspires in us a sense of the possible in our own lives.

Appendix: Some Namibian Terms and Expressions

With so many languages in play, many foreign words have become part of the local vernacular, whatever language is spoken. Here are some of them:

Ag: (pronounced as in German "ach") expression of frustration

Anderskleuriges: Afrikaans term for mixed-race people during *apartheid*

Bakkie: pickup truck

Bescherung: opening of gifts at Christmas (German)

Boeremusiek: Afrikaans music, most often accompanied on a concertina

Boeresports: Afrikaner sports activities

Boot, Bonnet, Tyres: car trunk, car hood, tires

Colored: mixed race

Gat vol: fed up

Gemsbok: oryx

Haoti: subdivisions of a Damara community

Igquira, igquirakazi: male and female witch doctor (Xhosa)

Is it?: expression used as a general response (e.g. "I don't have it in your size." Response: "Is it?")

Kappies: Voortrekker bonnet worn by Rehoboth Baster women

Lekker: I like it, fine

Lobola: bride price in traditional village; wedding ceremony in modern areas (Herero)

Moeg: tired of

Mooi: terrific

More: (pronounced "more-uh" with the "r" rolled) Good morning

Oom: older man (respectful, literally "uncle," Afrikaans)

Pack up: engine or other breakdown

Pad: road

Pad vark: road hog

Okuruuo: holy place of gathering (church, school, court of law)(Herero)

Olupale: meeting place near central fire (Ovambo)

Ompato: mother's clan (Ovambo)

Onganga: healer (Ovambo)

Opsitkers: A candle lit, in former times, by parents to determine how long a boyfriend could pay suit to their daughter (Afrikaans. "sit-up candle")

Oruzo: Himba ritual fire

Schneebantu: a Namibian-German term for Germans visiting from Germany

Sukkel: Namibian /Afrikaans word, to struggle or do battle

Tackie: tennis-type shoe

Tannie: older woman (Afrikaans, "auntie")

Trekboere: Boer trekkers—group of Afrikaners who moved up to Namibia and eventually to Angola to get away from everyone else

Tschers: Bye, from the English *Cheers* —spelled in German *Tjüs*

Where do you stay?: Where do you live?

Further Reading

Guedes, D., and P. Reiner. *The Letters of Emma Sarah Hahn: Pioneer Missionary among the Herero*. Windhoek: Namibia Scientific Society, 1992.

Henno, Martin. *The Sheltering Desert*. Hamburg: Two Books, 2002.

Hinz, Manfred O. *Without Chiefs There Would Be No Game*. Windhoek: Out of Africa Publishers, 2003.

Hubbard, Dianne (author), and Suzanne LaFont (ed.). *Unravelling Taboos: Gender and Sexuality in Namibia*. Windhoek: Legal Assistance Centre, 2007.

Jacobsohn, Margaret, Beverly and Peter Pickford. *Himba—Nomads of Africa*. Cape Town: Struik/New Holland, 2001.

Katjavivi, Peter H. *A History of Resistance in Namibia*, Paris: UNESCO Press/London: James Curry, 1988.

Melber, Henning (ed.), *Re-examining Liberation in Namibia: Political Cultures Since Independence*. Uppsala: Nordic Africa Institute, 2003.

Schoeman, Amy. *Skeleton Coast*. Cape Town: Struik/New Holland, 2003.

Seely, Mary, *The Namib: Natural History of an Ancient Desert*. 3rd ed., Windhoek: Desert Research Foundation of Namibia, 2004.

Stewart, Dianne. *Wisdom of Africa*. Cape Town: Struik/New Holland, 2005.

Thornberry, C. *A Nation Born—The Inside Story of Namibia's Independence*. Windhoek: Gamsberg Macmillan Publishers, 2004.

Useful Web Sites

http://www.namibiatourism.com.na/
(Information about the country, the people, the landscape)

http://www.travelnews.com.na/
(Features on Namibia, updated travel and conservation information)

http://www.holidaytravel.com.na/
(Yearbook of Namibian travel, with information on the country and its people)

http://www-sul.stanford.edu/africa/namibia.html
(Stanford University's impressive list of Web sites regarding Namibia)

http://www.tradedirectory.com.na/

http://www.namibweb.com/people.html
(A brief history of Namibia's peoples)

culture smart! namibia

Index

accommodation 136–7
African Union 45
Afrikaners 27–8, 58, 73, 81, 82, 158
agriculture 30–31, 39, 42–3, 46, 142
air travel 128–9, 130
Aloe dichotoma (quiver tree) 35
animal hides 111
animism 11, 50, 56
apartheid 2, 27, 33–4, 74, 78–9, 92
asylum seekers 45

bicycles 129
birds 122–3
birth control 60
Bismarck, Otto von 33
body language 158–9
border crossings 128
braaileis (*braai*) 74, 82, 86, 98, 99, 100
British 29
buses 135, 136
Bushmen *see* San/Bushmen
business cards 152
business community 142–4

Cao, Diego 32
Caprivi Strip 12–15, 30, 33, 119, 122, 126–7
Caprivians 11, 29–30, 73, 109
celebrations 73–5
cell phones 130, 133, 139, 159
character 46, 63, 79, 163
Chinese 30, 39, 142, 144
Christianity 11, 49, 50, 52, 53, 60
climate 10, 18–19
clothing
    appropriate dress 85–8
    buying 111, 113
    dress code 150–51
    indigenous 23, 24, 27, 50, 51, 72, 89
Colonial Wars (1904–07) 31
Coloreds 26, 27, 78
computers 160–61
conservation 8, 26, 36–8, 48, 119
constitution 56
contracts 155
corruption 146–7
couples, biracial and bicultural 78 9
crafts 30, 108–10, 142–3
crime 139
cuca bars 143
cultural sites 115, 116

daily life 95–6

Damara people 11, 25–6, 56, 69, 145
Damaraland 17, 25–6
dating 88–9
death and the afterlife 68–70
Development Bank of Namibia 141–2
diamond industry 36, 39, 40–41, 115, 144
Dias, Bartolomeu 32
dining out 105–6
Directorate of International Trade 141
disputes, settling 155, 157
drink 102
    drinking and driving 106, 132
driving 130–33, 134
drug use 107

economy 38–43, 140
education 24, 31, 40, 92–4, 96
entertaining business colleagues 152–3
entry requirements 128
environment 35–8, 48–9, 118, 163
Erongo 16
ethnic groups 9, 11, 19–30

fairy circles 15
family 31, 74, 76, 90–92
fire safety 99
fishing 30, 39, 42
folk wisdom 54–5
food 99–102, 103–4
foreigners, attitudes toward 80–81
Fredericks, Frankie 59–60, 117
friendships 76–7, 78, 163

galleries 116
gambling 106
gender relations 60–61
geography 8, 10, 12–13
German–Herero War (1904) 58, 59
Germany, Germans 17, 23, 28–9, 32–3, 58, 63, 66, 69, 74, 75, 81, 82, 101, 117, 143
getting to know Namibians 79–80
gifts 83, 153
Gobabis 16
government 11, 44, 140–42
grand apartheid 33–4, 78–9
greetings 81, 84, 151–2
Grootfontein 10, 16

handshake 72–3, 81, 83, 84, 151–2
Hardap 16
healing rituals 70–71

health 40, 45, 96, 138–9
Herero people 9, 11, 22–3, 25, 50, 53, 56, 58, 68, 72, 73, 85, 111, 145
Hereroland 17
heroes 57–60
Himba people 9, 23–4, 53, 61, 71, 72, 85, 89, 91, 95, 109, 111
history 32–5
hitchhiking 130, 133, 135
HIV/AIDS 61–2, 92, 93, 139
holidays and celebrations 73–5
"homelands" 17
homes 21–2, 90–91
homosexuality 61
hotels 137
humor 9, 157–8, 163
hunting 21, 64–7

independence (1990) 13, 26–7, 29, 31, 33, 34, 43, 58, 74, 142
Indians 30
insects 124–5
Internet 160, 161
invitations home 83–4
ivory 68, 111

jewelry 110–11, 112–13, 142
Jewish community 11, 30
Jordan, William Worthington 58
justice and social harmony 47–8

Kalahari Desert 8, 13
Kaokoland 16, 17, 68
Kapuuo, Clemens 58
Karas 16–17
Katima Mulilo 10, 15
Katutura township 34, 59, 74, 127
Kavango people 11, 15, 22, 52–3, 65–6, 69, 109, 117
Keetmanshoop 10, 16, 115
kissing 72, 81, 83
Kovango ethnic groups 11
Kunene 14
Kutako, Chief Hosea 59

land rights 31
language 9, 11, 27–8, 29, 35, 77, 78, 79, 92–3, 156–7, 158
Lubowski, Anton 58
Lüderitz 10, 16, 32
Maharero, Chief Samuel 58
making contact 148
making friends 88–9
Maltahöhe 16
Mandela, Nelson 34, 35, 44
Marenga, Captain Jacob 58
Mariental 16
marine life 121–2
marriage 50, 52, 72

matrilineal lineage 22
media 11, 161–2
medical care 96
meetings 154
military service 94
Ministry of Environment and Tourism (MET) 36, 37, 49, 77, 97
Ministry of Trade and Industry 140
Mpingana, Chief Nehale Iya 58
Mungunda, Mama Kakarakuze 59
museums 114–16
music 116–17
Muslim community 11, 52

Nama people (Hottentots) 11, 24–5, 51, 53, 65, 68, 69, 110, 115, 116
Namib Desert 8, 12, 35, 57, 115, 125
Namibia Chamber of Commerce and Industry 150
Namibia in Africa 43–5
Namibia Trade Directory 149
Namibian Investment Centre (NIC) 141
Namibian terms and expressions 164
Namilish 157, 158
national parks 14, 16, 17, 36–7, 49, 74, 116, 119, 121, 122, 126, 127, 137–8
natural resources 25–8
nature, attitudes toward 48–9, 118, 163
Ndemufayo, Chief Mandume ya 59
negotiations 154–5
NGOs 37, 119, 120, 142, 143
Nguvauva, Chief Kahimemua 58
nightlife 106
nonconfrontation 46, 63, 157
Nujoma, Sam 34–5, 57, 146–7

Offshore Development Company 141
Ohangwena region 13–14
Okahandja 10, 16, 75
Okakarara 16
Okambahe 75
Okavango 12, 13
Omaheke 16
Omaruru 109
Omusati region 13–14
Ondangwa 10, 14
Ondonga 58
Ongwediva 14
Opuwo 14
Oranjemund 10
Oshakati 10, 14

60 Winter Street
Keene, NH 03431
352-0157

Oshana region 13–14
Oshikoto region 13–14
Otjiwarongo 10, 120
Otjozondjupa 16
Ovakwambi people 59
Ovambo people 9, 11, 21–2, 44, 52, 54–5, 61, 64–5, 68, 69, 71, 72–3, 109, 111, 117, 145
Ovambo regions 13–14

patrilineal lineage 22, 24
personal relationships 148–50
personal space and privacy 63, 79, 92
petit apartheid 78
plants 125
Pohamba, Hifikepunye 35
political parties 43
population 8, 11
"Portuguese stores" 143
presentations 154
private preserves 138
public holidays 74
public transport 129–30
punctuality 153

racial diversity 144–5
radio 11, 161–2
rail travel 135–6
Red Line 17–18
regions 13–18
Rehoboth 10
Rehoboth Basters 11, 26–7, 69, 75, 78
religion 11, 49–53, 56
reptiles 123–4
respect 73, 157
restaurants 105, 152
rites of passage 71
road travel 130–33
Rundu 10, 15

safety 139
San/Bushmen 11, 15, 20–21, 32, 36, 56, 65, 70, 71, 110, 116, 117
shopping for pleasure 107–11, 113–14
Skeleton Coast 8, 16, 120
Small Business Credit Guarantee Trust 141
smoking 84, 106
South Africa (main references) 17, 27, 28, 33

South Africa Development Community (SADC) 45
South African rule 13, 17, 33–4, 146
South West Africa 32, 33
South West Africa People's Organization (SWAPO) 34, 39, 44, 74, 145
souvenirs 114
sports 117–18
storytelling 68
street beggars 107
street vendors 107–8
summer vacations 96–7
Swakopmund 10, 16, 75, 97, 106, 110, 118, 127

table manners 83–4
taxis 136
Team Namibia 147
technology 160–61
telecommunications 11, 130, 133, 139, 159–60
television 11, 161
time 11
  attitudes toward 63
  punctuality 153
  in a social setting 81–2
tourism 26, 37–40, 119, 142
tours 135–6
tribal differences 31
Tshilongo, Chief Ipumbu ya 59
Tsumeb 10
Tsumkwe 16
Tswana people 11, 30
Twyfelfontein 14, 20, 126

unifying symbols 56–7
Uukwambi people 64–5

Walvis Bay 10, 16, 28, 29, 33, 123, 127
water ceremonies 67
Welwitschia mirabilis 35
widows 48, 60
wildlife 15, 19, 26, 35, 36, 37, 65–7, 118–25, 131
Windhoek 8, 10, 16, 52, 75, 94, 105, 108, 109, 110, 114, 115, 117, 118, 127, 129, 138, 143
Witbooi, Kaptein Hendrik 58
women in business 145–6
work ethic 153, 163

Acknowledgments

Thanks to Elena Torreguitar, PhD, Dr. Geoff Maughan-Brown, Ute Maughan-Brown, Amy Schoeman, and Ambassador Piero De Masi.